A
LIFE
THAT
LEADS
———

PURSUING CHRIST AND
IMPACTING OTHERS

A LIFE THAT LEADS

JOSH BENADUM

100 MOVEMENTS
PUBLISHING

First published in 2026 by 100Movements Publishing
www.100Movements.com
© 2026 by Josh Benadum

The author has no responsibility for the persistence or accuracy of URLs for external or third-party internet websites referred to in this book and does not guarantee that any content on such websites is, or will remain, accurate or appropriate.

Some names have been changed to protect the privacy of individuals.

Library of Congress Control Number: 2026902671

All Scripture quotations, unless otherwise indicated, are from Holy Bible, New International Version®, NIV®. Copyright © 1973, 1978, 1984, 2011 by Biblica, Inc.™ Used by permission of Zondervan. All rights reserved worldwide. www.zondervan.com. The "NIV" and "New International Version" are trademarks registered in the United States Patent and Trademark Office by Biblica, Inc.™

Scripture quotations marked CSB are taken from the Christian Standard Bible®, Copyright © 2017 by Holman Bible Publishers. Used by permission. Christian Standard Bible® and CSB® are federally registered trademarks of Holman Bible Publishers.

Scripture quotations marked NASB are taken from the (NASB®) New American Standard Bible®, Copyright © 1960, 1971, 1977, 1995, 2020 by The Lockman Foundation. Used by permission. All rights reserved. lockman.org.

Scripture quotations marked NASB1995 are taken from the (NASB®) New American Standard Bible®, Copyright © 1995 by The Lockman Foundation. Used by permission. All rights reserved. lockman.org.

Scripture quotations marked NLT are taken from the *Holy Bible*, New Living Translation, copyright © 1996, 2004, 2015 by Tyndale House Foundation. Used by permission of Tyndale House Publishers, Carol Stream, Illinois 60188. All rights reserved.

Scripture quotations marked NKJV are taken from the New King James Version®. Copyright © 1982 by Thomas Nelson. Used by permission. All rights reserved.

Unless otherwise stated, all emphasis in Scripture quotations is the author's own.

ISBN 978-1-955142-75-5 (print)
ISBN 978-1-955142-76-2 (eBook)

Cover design and interior illustrations by Jude May

100Movements Publishing
An imprint of 100Movements
Cody, Wyoming
www.100Movements.com

How can we be the leaders that God calls us to be? That's what I love about Josh Benadum's *A Life That Leads*. It juggles the tensions between character and competence, so we can cultivate both the soul and the skills required to be a leader. This is a book for anyone wanting to transform their inner life and their outward leadership.

SAM CHAN, fellow, The Keller Center for Cultural Apologetics;
head trainer and mentor, EvQ school of evangelism, City Bible Forum;
author, *How to Talk About Jesus (Without Being THAT Guy)*

Like Josh himself, this book is both thoughtful and wise. In it, he paints a beautiful and balanced picture of healthy Christian leadership, inviting us into the confluence of character, competency, and intimacy with God—a great resource for everyday Christian leaders.

BRIAN SANDERS, founder, Underground Network;
author, *The 6 Seasons of Calling*

In this well-written book, Josh Benadum presents leadership as a spiritual vocation rather than a professional role. He calls readers to cultivate the interior life from which enduring influence springs, envisioning leadership as an act of love, alignment, and creative service for the sake of the world.

ALAN HIRSCH, author of numerous award-winning books on missional
spirituality, leadership, and organization; cofounder, Movement Leaders
Collective and Forge Missional Training Network

This book is a gift to the countless men and women who quietly shape the church through faithful presence rather than public platforms. Rooted in Scripture but grounded in real life, it reminds us that becoming like Jesus is both God's work and our daily yes. Benadum writes with humility and honesty, offering practical, accessible guidance that is deeply helpful for everyday disciples faithfully leading where God has placed them.

KATHRYN MAACK, founder and visionary, Dwellings; coauthor,
Whole: The Lifechanging Power of Relating to God with All of Yourself

I had the privilege of coaching Josh during his church-planting journey, and what struck me then still strikes me now: He leads from a place of deep humility, genuine care, and a steady commitment to form people into the likeness of Christ. *A Life That Leads* reflects the way he actually lives and shepherds others. This book will help every believer see leadership as something rooted in character, presence, and everyday faithfulness.

SAM CHACKO, lead pastor, LOFT City Church; director of startup coaching, Stadia Church Planting; executive director, Plant Dallas

What I love about Josh's writing is that it's not just instructive; it's wildly practical. It feels like a training manual for forming the kind of character that will develop elders within our networks. It's not only full of wisdom gathered from his years of studying Scripture—it also gets at the practices that will actually form leaders. You can read this book like a field guide and then keep returning to it as you cultivate leadership in your own life.

BRIAN JOHNSON, founding leader and hub director, Kansas City Underground

In contemporary leadership, many are concerned about how we lead, while God is more concerned about how we live. *A Life That Leads* pivots us aright! Godly leadership does not operate on its own terms. As such, Josh Benadum offers a biblical compass for the discipleship of leaders. Most significantly, he shows us that the first call of leadership is not just to advance the kingdom; it is to abide in the King so that the kingdom might truly be advanced!

EDMUND CHAN, founder and leadership mentor, Global Alliance of Intentional Disciplemaking Churches

A Life That Leads is a compelling reminder that true Christian leadership is not built on charisma or methods but on the faithful formation of Christlike character. Grounded in Scripture and decades of disciple-making experience, Josh Benadum reframes leadership not as something to be achieved but as something we become through faithful obedience to Christ. This is an essential read for everyday believers who long to make a lasting impact for Jesus.

CONRAD HILARIO, senior pastor, Dwell Community Church; author, *Searching for Wisdom: Finding the Father in Proverbs*

For my parents, Tim and Marjie Benadum: Thank you for your faith and courage in selling everything and moving our family to Cambodia, teaching us by example that the joy of following Christ is worth every sacrifice.

And for my lovely wife and partner in all things, Meri: Everything I do is better because of you.

And for our children, Thea, Iris, and Isak.

Contents

Foreword

A few months ago, I had the joy of ministering alongside Josh Benadum in Cambodia, where we were the speakers at a conference. Josh had brought a team of volunteers from his church who ran the children's program. While enjoying comradeship with Josh, I was also deeply encouraged by the servant spirit and Christlike attitude of his team members. It was clear that they had been discipled well. So, when Josh later told me he was writing a book on leadership, I was keen to read the work of a man who had already proven his principles in the lives of his team.

In our current culture, Christian thinking about leadership has been hijacked by unbiblical emphases, often focusing on ability, pragmatic effectiveness, and position. Many writers on leadership have been more influenced by the world's thinking than by Scripture. Ability and giftedness are indeed important in the biblical understanding of leadership, but they are not primary. The primary focus is on character, as clearly evidenced in Paul's lists of qualifications for leaders in the Pastoral Epistles—which this book explores.

Christian leadership is a means of influencing people toward God's will by way of example, teaching, caring, and directing. Therefore, reading a book on Christian leadership should leave us yearning to be more Christlike so that we can guide those we lead toward grasping God's will for their lives. When this happens, the organization or church to which they belong also thrives and moves forward.

This book has the potential to nurture a thirst for more of God in your life, equipping you to influence others in a Godward direction. As a result, those you lead—whether one or many—will move into seasons of growth and fresh exploits for God.

May you be refreshed, edified, instructed, and motivated as you read this book.

Ajith Fernando
Teaching Director, Youth for Christ, Sri Lanka; author,
Discipling in a Multicultural World

Introduction

When you hear the phrase "Christian leader," what comes to mind? Is it a famous theologian who has shaped modern thought, like C. S. Lewis? Or perhaps a more contemporary thinker, like Tim Keller? You might think of powerful preachers whose words have moved millions, like Billy Graham or Francis Chan; or pioneering missionaries whose legacies are still felt a century later, like Amy Carmichael, Sundar Singh, and Hudson Taylor. These men and women had monumental influence for the kingdom, and God continues to raise up many more like them.

But this book is not about those exceptional few.

Instead, this book is written for each and every disciple of Jesus. For most of us, our names will never be known outside our relatively small and immediate circles. The most widespread and pervasive force for kingdom change is not accomplished by the celebrated few who make it to the stage or screen. God's mission goes forward because everyday disciples live, share, talk about, and demonstrate the love of Jesus in their neighborhoods, colleges, and workplaces. This is exactly how the early church spread and challenged the broken systems of their own day—providing hope and a compelling model for how we might do the same. Talking about the early church, missiologist

Edward L. Smither states, "While there were full-time missionaries, this seems to be the exception more than the norm…. Everyday Christians were also convinced of the priority of mission…. Mission was not the work of a specialized group; rather, it was the responsibility of every Christian."[1] The call and the mission are for each one of us.

God doesn't just move through those who are obviously gifted or privileged. He calls people in every place from every background, fills us with his Spirit, and uses our efforts for eternal impact. Paul reminded the Corinthians of this:

> Brothers and sisters, think of what you were when you were called. Not many of you were wise by human standards; not many were influential; not many were of noble birth. But God chose the foolish things of the world to shame the wise; God chose the weak things of the world to shame the strong.
>
> 1 CORINTHIANS 1:26–27

Stop for a moment and consider this: Who have been the most influential Christians in your own life? Chances are, most of them aren't leading a global nonprofit or have a million followers. More likely, they were a consistent mentor, a patient coach, a dedicated friend, or a family member whose quiet faithfulness taught you more than any viral video sermon ever could. Their influence wasn't from their title; it was the substance of their life. If we are to become that kind of influential person to others, then we must have a similar substance to our own lives: Christlike character. That's what it means to live a life that leads—relying not on our talents or charisma but allowing every part of our lives to be shaped by Jesus and for our character to become the channel through which his transforming power flows to others.

Contemporary society urgently needs men and women who reflect the mental, emotional, ethical, and moral traits of Jesus.

While we have reached new peaks of material comfort and technological advancement, many of us are simultaneously grappling with a profound crisis of despair, fueled by the gap between the curated perfection of "screen lives" and the messy, authentic reality of human experience. This crisis is visible in the data. The World Happiness Report recently revealed a historic reversal: Young adults in North America and Western Europe are now less happy than their elders, with high rates of anxiety and loneliness replacing optimism.[2] In a culture saturated with constant connectivity yet starving for genuine community, the simple, enduring hope offered through Christ and mediated through the faithful lives of his people is vital. We need many more believers to become genuine disciples who make disciples if we are to fulfill the Great Commission. This mission is the global, ongoing work of multiplication—extending this life-giving hope, as followers of Christ bring the gospel to every person in every place.

Why I Wrote This Book

As a disciple-maker and community builder for seventeen years, I've focused on training, equipping, and sending out disciples for ministry in every sphere of life. So, I have seen firsthand the extraordinary things that seemingly ordinary people can accomplish through the power of the Holy Spirit. But through my work overseeing networks of house churches and partnering with organizations like Youth for Christ, Stadia Church Planting, and Brave Future (a research collaboration dedicated to the future of the church), I often encounter a perceived tension facing people who are trying to serve God. They often feel caught between two essential goals: effective ministry (skill) and maintaining their own spiritual depth (soul). This tension is often created and reinforced by books and training materials. Strategy materials focus on skills and often treat disciple-making and ministry in general like a business model, with tips, tricks, and best practices to maximize numerical growth. Spiritual growth resources, on the other hand, pay attention to the soul and are often highly contemplative, abstract, and focused on the inner, reflective life. The development of skill and the formation of soul are presented as separate or even opposed. This makes it challenging for leaders to integrate them into one cohesive, holistic approach that nurtures their own spiritual depth while still pursuing effective service to God.

However, the biblical truth is that our inner transformation and the impact we have on others are intimately related. We can aim for *both* deep, robust personal discipleship *and* wide-reaching ministry impact at the same time. Jesus didn't have to choose between these goals, and neither do we. The aim of this book is to help you chart a clearer course toward a dynamic spiritual life that also decisively leads. It's about pursuing the character traits of Jesus and developing the correlated skills that will make us enduringly fruitful.

The Journey Ahead

The ultimate purpose of this book is to help you discover your crucial part in the unfolding of God's kingdom movement. This means accepting that spiritual leadership is for everyone, in different spheres of influence. We are all called to serve and participate in making disciples (Matthew 28:19), and we must learn to do this intentionally.

Scripture has a lot to say about how ordinary Christian leaders are called and formed. In the pages to come, we'll explore God's wisdom through three distinct parts: In part one, we chart the essential elements of God's call, your foundational identity, and the necessity of abiding in Christ. In part two, we dive into key aspects of Christlike character and how these traits can be expressed through tangible practices. Finally, in part three, we address how to maintain spiritual health for the long haul and grow your influence through the essential union of character and competency.

This book is not about pursuing a grand, unsustainable vision. It's about becoming a person who lives out the fullness of Christ wherever you are called and with whomever you are walking. Let's get started and marvel together at how Jesus empowers us to influence others along the way!

PART ONE

FORMING A LIFE THAT LEADS

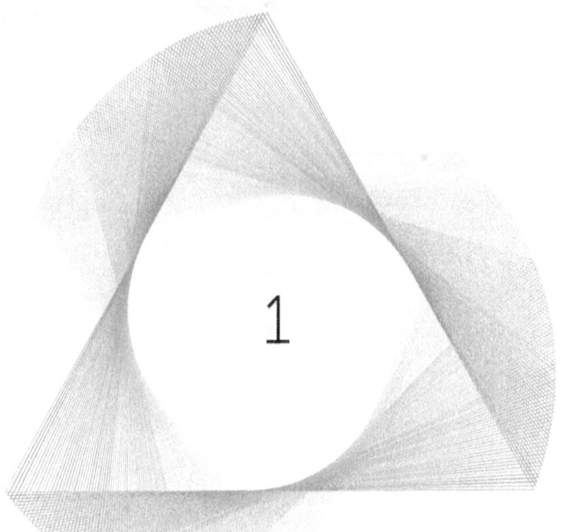

1

The Making of a Leader

One Faithful Step After Another

Vision leads to venture, and history is on the side of
venturesome faith. The person of vision takes fresh
steps of faith across gullies and chasms.

J. OSWALD SANDERS

I'LL NEVER FORGET the multiday hike I took through the French
Alps with my dad and brother. It was the most strenuous thing I'd
ever done, with thousands of feet of climbing and descending each
day. Every time we started a new ascent, the peak looked impossibly
far away. You know that feeling—when the goal seems so distant, you
wonder if you'll ever get there?

But we didn't stop. We just kept putting one foot in front of the
other. The most breathtaking moments weren't when we reached a
mountain pass, but when we stopped, turned around, and saw how
far we'd come just by keeping our eyes on the path in front of us and
plodding forward.

I am convinced that most of us arrive at spiritual leadership the same way. Few of us know the scope of God's plan for our lives and ministry. At times, some of us receive prophecies or visions that confirm our life trajectory. But, by and large, we get where God wants us to go simply by taking consistent steps and saying yes again and again.

We don't set out with a crystal-clear vision of what we are supposed to accomplish. Instead, we discover our path incrementally as we grow in faith and explore new directions. Spiritual leadership isn't primarily a position you achieve but a person you become, one faithful step after another. True leadership is found in the kind of life we live—a life that leads by pursuing Christ and letting his work in us overflow to others.

The Unpredictable Path to Spiritual Growth

I used to think of Christian growth and life in general as a linear process: You work hard, you succeed. After deciding to follow Jesus when I was eighteen, I knew I'd face some setbacks. But I was confident I would triumph over my problems and even the problems of others. No question about it.

I genuinely handed over the direction of my life, believing God would give me something better in return. I loved Christian community and devoured everything I could about the Bible. I even began to see real fruit in my efforts to serve others. But looking back, I realize I was still entitled and driven by self-will. Though I wanted to follow God, I was doing it on my own terms. I viewed spiritual growth like earning a college degree—with enough effort, I'd eventually become an expert who no longer needed to go back to school.

But life turned out to be a lot less linear than I'd hoped.

Six years into my walk with Jesus and one year into marriage, everything started to unravel. My job and my leadership role in the church were on the line. But more importantly, my young marriage was in peril. I felt broken, frustrated, and completely out of control.

Sitting on a park bench, I poured my heart out to my friend and mentor, Dave. He had listened to me vent countless times before and was always empathic, ready with good advice. But this time, his message and tone were different.

"You know, Josh," he said. "I have seen a lot of leaders come and go. Many are gifted and talented. But what differentiates spiritual men and women is how they respond to moments like these. You can't expect to have a significant impact for God without encountering real suffering that develops your character."

Like a perfectly tuned guitar string, those words rang true and have been ringing in my head ever since. That moment was a turning point, the beginning of a paradigm shift I believe God was birthing in me.

The Deeper Purpose

As it turns out, I am not entitled to success on my own terms. None of us are. And that's true even when it comes to good and godly initiatives. As the prophet Isaiah explains, God, the Creator, is the Potter, and we are the clay (Isaiah 45:9). He has the absolute right to do whatever he chooses with the lump of clay. But we aren't just at the mercy of a capricious Potter. The apostle Paul states that "our present sufferings are not worth comparing with the glory that will be revealed in us" (Romans 8:18) and that "in all things God works for the good of those who love him, who have been called according to his purpose" (Romans 8:28). Even if we are broken down, taken apart, and re-formed, it is for God's loving purposes. He is making those he loves into something new.

God gets to call the shots and is under no obligation to give us what we want or what we think we deserve. But he loves us. He is good. We can trust him no matter what happens. This dual truth—God's total sovereignty and his ultimate goodness—sets us free. It allows us to relinquish our entitlement and illusions of control, knowing there is no final reason to be afraid if this is really what God is like.

When God allows circumstances that force us into detours or difficulties, it can feel painful, unproductive, or inefficient. But if we embrace this, it's in precisely these times he draws us into a place where we learn to know him deeply. God's central goal for your life (and mine) isn't just maximum comfort and productivity. It's not even leadership. What the beautiful, infinite God of the universe wants more than anything is for us to profoundly know Jesus and, as an overflow of that knowledge, to become like him. *The endgame of the Christian life is to become like Jesus.* On our own, and even at our best, this is an outcome we could never hope to achieve. But he is absolutely dedicated to accomplishing his will in our lives.

As author, missionary, and pastor J. Oswald Sanders once wrote, the ultimate goal of the Christian life is to "attain in ever-increasing degree the standard of spiritual maturity which was seen in perfection in Christ."[1] Being formed in the image of Jesus is the ultimate goal of the Christian life. This purpose underpins everything—from our personal spiritual growth to our service and leadership.

Okay, great life lesson, you might be thinking. *But what does all this have to do with being called to lead?*

Good question. Christlike character is every Christian's first calling. Sure, God may give us specific roles, but our primary calling is always to be formed by Jesus.

The modern world, particularly in the West, often encourages us to find our "special calling" through personality tests and self-help seminars. Although much of this can be well-intentioned and even helpful, it can also lead us to unbiblical forms of leadership. We are taught that our value lies in securing a unique leadership role or in our gifts or accomplishments.

But our true identity isn't rooted in a "special" calling; it's anchored in what Jesus already did for us. This means that even if tragedy or circumstances limit our gifts, we can still be fruitful and fulfilled—because those things are found in Jesus.

It's supposed to be more about *him* than it is about *us*.

When we view Christlike character formation—the process theologians call "sanctification"—as our first and ongoing calling, it makes sense that God would forgo what we might see as "progress" for the sake of his higher objective: transformation! God's primary goal for us isn't to make us great leaders; it's to make us like his Son.

I learned this the hard way. Without God changing me, my marriage would have been toast. What's more, I wouldn't have been ready for the future ways he wanted me to serve. God was refining me but also preparing me for what came next. God forms us gradually as we respond one faithful step at a time to our primary and common calling. Special roles and opportunities may come as we grow in both character and necessary skills, but it's our character that matters most to God. As we seek to grow and help others do the same, it's important we understand and accept his priorities.

This completely changes how you approach your own leadership development. Simply cramming your brain with information won't magically make you a great leader. A certificate may prove your knowledge, but it won't give you courage. A conference may inspire, but it won't make you wise. Instead, courage is a quality that accumulates in the life of a person who decides to trust God more and more (Joshua 1:9). Wisdom comes through receiving and obeying God's commands with an attitude of awe and reverence (Proverbs 1:7). Becoming a leader isn't just about what you learn; it's about the person you're being shaped into.

Jesus understood this. He spent the bulk of his time on earth doing life-on-life discipleship with a small group of friends. Discipleship for Jesus wasn't some slick, well-branded six-week program. Jesus and his disciples walked long distances together. They talked over meals and discussed God's ways late into the night. They went to synagogue, weddings, and festivals as a group. Jesus intentionally built deep relationship with his disciples through these shared, intimate moments, relating to their messy human struggles and modeling the very transformation he called them toward. Along the way, he taught them and sent them out to apply what they learned.

Jesus wasn't just teaching the disciples. He was forming them.

Deep transformation—the kind that makes a person a real leader—happens through this sort of heavy relational investment, not just sitting in a classroom.

The church desperately needs more leaders, and not just people with a title or a seminary degree. There's a shortage of ordinary, authentic leaders—everyday men and women who are willing to make disciples right where they are, in every part of society.[2]

You might think of a leader as someone with a specific role or position. But Jesus completely flipped that idea on its head, teaching that the greatest among us are servants (Matthew 23:11). True leadership, then, is about finding ways to serve others. This kind of leadership isn't a special skill or a gift for a select few; instead, it is the natural overflow of what God has done and is doing in us. It's about Christlike character that is formed through a painstaking, spiritually empowered, holistic process. You can't just learn about it from a book; you have to let it be worked into you—and walk it out with the people he's placed in your life.

The Journey Ahead

The good news is that this path is much like my hike in the Alps. You don't need a perfect map for the entire journey. When it comes to life, you can't possibly know what challenges you will face. But God shows us what we need to know in order to take the next faithful steps. So, how do you get started?

Christian literature on character and leadership is often vague and impractical. And so we will try to move beyond theory and get to practical, actionable insights. We'll dive into what this means by exploring the nature of the journey (understanding what character formation truly is), the process of transformation (discovering how this growth actually happens), and your role (learning how to participate in your own growth and help others do the same). We'll also address some of the important biblical tensions, such as: Why does God often seem to choose and use flawed individuals to lead his people? What's the real connection between character and the ability to lead? Is it possible to have good character but be uninfluential?

Ultimately, I hope this book will empower you to take that simple but significant next step, so that one day you can look back in awe at how far you've come.

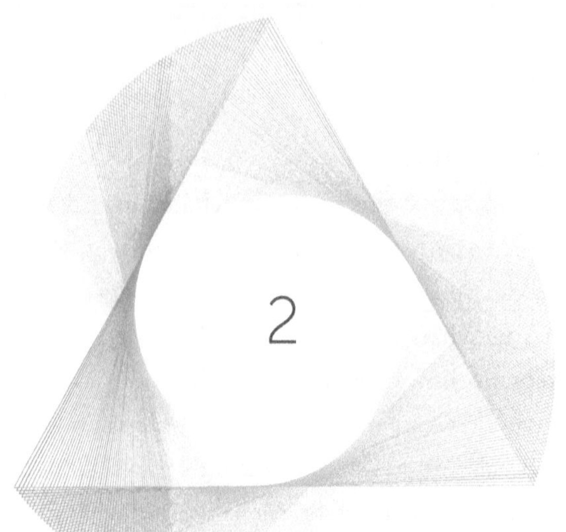

The Goal of the Christian Life

Becoming Like Jesus

> "I am going to the King's City," said little Christian.
> "Won't you come with me?"
> **LITTLE PILGRIM'S PROGRESS** BY HELEN L. TAYLOR

I'M A BIG fan of the old American comic strip *Calvin and Hobbes*. Calvin's nerdy dad is all about character, often lecturing Calvin and connecting character to everything Calvin finds boring or distasteful, such as eating broccoli or doing his chores. I hope to avoid that dynamic with my own children! But for many, the very idea of building character feels exactly like that—a pushy, moralistic lecture that's detached from real life. The word has become vague, a free-floating concept with no objective standard.

And yet, despite our modern confusion, people of every time, place, and walk of life have realized how much character matters. The Merriam-Webster dictionary defines character as "the complex of mental and ethical traits marking and often individualizing a person, group, or nation."[1] George Washington, military commander and first president of the United States, advised his nephew, "good moral character is the first essential in a man.... It is therefore highly important that you should endeavor not only to be learned but virtuous."[2] Bruce Lee, a celebrated warrior in his own right, once remarked, "Knowledge will give you power, but character respect."[3]

But for the follower of Jesus, character is more than just polite norms or a culturally conditioned set of virtues. It's not just a way to win admiration, a personal self-improvement project, or the grit you develop through doing hard things. Character, for the Christian, is defined by an external set of objective values that serve as a common measuring stick. That measuring stick is the person of Jesus, who is the very image or pattern of God Almighty (Colossians 1:15).

Character is the way we express Christlikeness. So, let's adapt Merriam-Webster's definition to suit our purposes: "Good character" refers to how a person embodies the mental, emotional, ethical, and moral traits of Jesus. True character transformation involves becoming in every way like our Savior, Jesus Christ. As we pursue Christ, our lives are gradually transformed. This transformation is not just for our own sake, but so that we can impact others—living a life that leads.

Incredibly, Scripture teaches that anyone who has God's Spirit indwelling and activated within them is already involved in this supernatural transformation. Paul captures this truth when he writes, "And we all, who with unveiled faces contemplate the

Lord's glory, are being transformed into his image with ever-increasing glory, which comes from the Lord, who is the Spirit" (2 Corinthians 3:18).

In the coming chapters, we will explore how this transformation is not a solitary endeavor. Yes, it does require times of quiet contemplation, alone with God. But the Spirit also uses the community of believers to shape us, as we learn from one another, encourage one another, and hold each other accountable. Dietrich Bonhoeffer, in his classic *Life Together*, insists that both the "day together," as well as the "day alone" are essential for robust formation.[4] Both are necessary if we are to become what God intends.

This pervasive spiritual transformation—pursuing Christ both alone and together—is synonymous with spiritual maturity. Maturity implies a progression, and this movement from immaturity to maturity is the very process that prepares us for leadership. A one-year sapling is just as much a tree as a fifty-year-old mighty oak, but over time, the oak fulfills the potential of what a tree can be. Its branches grow thicker, its roots deeper, its canopy wider, and it begins to bear acorns. Similarly, spiritually maturing leaders grow strong themselves, but in their fullest form produce new life.

Likewise, I was just as much a Christian the day I received Jesus into my life as I am today. But through God's power and mercy, there has been considerable growth. There is a critical distinction, however: A tree is a passive beneficiary of naturally occurring circumstances, but we have a designated part to play in our own maturing. I'll talk about that more in the next chapter.

The Biblical Evidence

It's a bold claim to say that any one thing is the primary goal of the Christian life. There are many worthy objectives and meaningful pursuits involved in following the Lord of all things. But the Bible gives us a clear answer: The ultimate goal is a lifelong pursuit of an intimate relationship with Christ that results in being transformed into his likeness (Romans 8:29). This isn't just one goal among many; it's the one that ties everything together and gives our lives a single, clear purpose. So, let's consider the biblical evidence for this truth.

Paul's Pursuit of Christlikeness

Before meeting Jesus, Paul lived a life of worldly success—a top-tier scholar and a man of great social, religious, and political esteem. But on the road to Damascus, Jesus turned this man's life upside down and shook out the contents. Paul reevaluated his entire life and its purpose, writing in Philippians 3:

> But whatever were gains to me I now consider loss for the sake of Christ. What is more, I consider everything a loss because of the surpassing worth of knowing Christ Jesus my Lord, for whose sake I have lost all things.... I press on to take hold of that for which Christ Jesus took hold of me. Brothers and sisters, I do not consider myself yet to have taken hold of it. But one thing I do: Forgetting what is behind and straining toward what is ahead, I press on toward the goal to win the prize for which God has called me heavenward in Christ Jesus.
>
> PHILIPPIANS 3:7–8, 12–14

Paul's life was now defined and motivated by a relationship. He would still strive and press forward (Paul was a driven man by nature), but now with a singular purpose: to know Christ more and more, and in that knowledge, to become like him: "[taking] hold of that for which Christ took hold of [him]." It was true for him, and it's true for us. Anything of ultimate worth, whether it be knowledge, purpose, or even love, comes through knowing and being known by Jesus.

It's easy to look at Paul and think he was a special "spiritual person" with a unique calling. But Paul didn't just stumble across a purely personal truth in his Damascus Road encounter. Instead, he learned something about God's gift and desire for every person. When he writes to the Colossians, he explains that he admonishes and teaches everyone "so that we may present everyone fully mature in Christ" (Colossians 1:28). Though Paul had never met these believers, he was committed to helping others pursue the very same goal.

In fact, we need others to run alongside us if we expect to get where God wants us to go. Paul urged Timothy to "pursue righteousness, faith, love and peace, along with those who call on the Lord out of a pure heart" (2 Timothy 2:22). Hebrews tells us we can "run with perseverance the race marked out for us" precisely because we are surrounded by "a great cloud of witnesses" (Hebrews 12:1). The Bible knows nothing of lone-wolf spirituality. True Jesus-followers live connected, and a big part of this involves consistently praying for one another and investing in each other's growth.

I don't know about you, but when I pray for others, I tend to focus on their specific problems. But Paul's prayers were markedly different. He didn't primarily pray for believers' circumstances, but for their spiritual maturity—for a deeper, transformative work in their inner being that would allow them to be filled with the fullness of God. His focus was on the depth of their relationship with God, and that they would increasingly realize all the riches they have through him. This pursuit of divine closeness that results in fulfillment and power is precisely what we see in Paul's prayer in Ephesians 3:14–19:

> For this reason I kneel before the Father, from whom every family in heaven and on earth derives its name. I pray that out of his glorious riches he may strengthen you with power through his Spirit in your inner being, so that Christ may dwell in your hearts through faith. And I pray that you, being rooted and established in love, may have power, together with all the Lord's holy people, to grasp how wide and long and high and deep is the love of Christ, and to know this love that surpasses knowledge—that you may be filled to the measure of all the fullness of God.

Paul's prayers teach us that everything we need in the Christian life, including the capacity to serve others, flows from a growing relationship with Jesus. So, we ought to make our connection with him our highest priority. This is exactly what Paul calls us to in his letter to the Romans.

> Therefore, I urge you, brothers and sisters, in view of God's mercy, to offer your bodies as a living sacrifice, holy and pleasing to God—this is your true and proper worship. Do not conform to the pattern of this world, but be transformed by the renewing of your mind. Then you will be able to test and approve what God's will is—his good, pleasing and perfect will.
>
> ROMANS 12:1–2

When we offer our whole life to God, it doesn't just lead to good behavior; it initiates a process of profound inner change: personal transformation. The Greek word here for "transformed" is μεταμορφόω (*metamorphoó*), meaning "to change inwardly in fundamental character or condition."[5]

Notice again how the biblical paradigm is that this happens together. Corporate worship isn't just about singing songs. If that were the case, a flourishing Christian life would only require an uplifting chord progression and semi-weekly attendance. The real thing involves heart-level reorientation for the entire community toward the will of God. The collective process of becoming like Jesus forms a powerful, transformative network!

Drawing from Colossians 1:28–29 and Ephesians 4:13, J. Oswald Sanders concludes that "the goal of the Christian life is to attain in ever-increasing degree the standard of spiritual maturity which was seen in perfection in Christ."[6] Likewise, John Stott, the influential Anglican theologian and author wrote in his final address, "What is God's purpose for his people? ... I want to share with you where my mind has come to rest as I approach the end of my pilgrimage here on earth. It is this: God wants his people to become like Christ."[7] As evidence, Stott cites Romans 8:29, which urges predestined believers to "be conformed to the image of his Son, that he might be the firstborn among many brothers and sisters."

Becoming like Christ goes way beyond simply trying to live as a moral person. Embodying the character of Jesus requires learning his humility (Philippians 2:5–8), his service (John 13:14–15), his love (Ephesians 5:2), and his endurance (1 Peter 2:18–21). It is the daily adoption of his mission as our own (John 20:21).[8] Full-orbed change like this requires the life-giving work of the Holy Spirit. Ultimately, Christlike character is the practical fulfillment of the two greatest commandments: love for God and love for neighbor (Mark 12:30–31). We'll explore what this looks like practically in part two.

Why the Goal Matters

Why go to all this trouble to define the goal of the Christian life? Imagine a hiker on a long trail. How important is it that she knows where she's going? It couldn't matter more! Exact knowledge of her destination is everything. It's the objective that sets her pace, measures her rations, and even determines her equipment. If she gets it wrong, the cost is monumental. At best, she'll be lost and wandering; at worst, she might die of starvation or exposure.

The stakes on our spiritual journey are even higher. If we assume that being a Christian should lead to financial prosperity, we're likely to feel disillusioned and question our faith if we lose our job or face financial hardship. Or, if we think following Jesus guarantees a life without pain or difficulty, we may struggle with our faith when we experience illness, a failed relationship, or other tragedies.

It's dangerous to confuse our true goal with temporary things like happiness and personal success. Christians who even subtly believe that these are the promised outcomes of spiritual living are extremely vulnerable and will never develop the wisdom or endurance needed to lead in a broken world. Sadly, many believers fall into doubt and begin deconstructing their faith, simply because they are using the wrong map for the Christian life.

Elisabeth Elliot's husband was murdered while trying to bring the gospel to a remote tribe in the Amazon. Years later, Elisabeth returned to this same tribe, extending radical forgiveness alongside the message of Jesus. In her book *Be Still My Soul*, she says, "Nothing takes Him by surprise. Nothing is for nothing. His plan is to make me holy, and hardship is indispensable for that as long as I live in this hard old world."[9] Her focus on becoming like Jesus allowed her to turn to God and to grow, even through one of the worst experiences imaginable. As a result, she was formed into one of the most joyful and resilient leaders of her generation.

Thank God his true intentions for his children are infinitely more secure than our earthly hopes and dreams! When becoming like Christ is the goal, we are free to navigate life in a fallen world with hope and purpose. Living toward this single, unifying goal is what turns an ordinary person into a leader of remarkable and inspiring character.

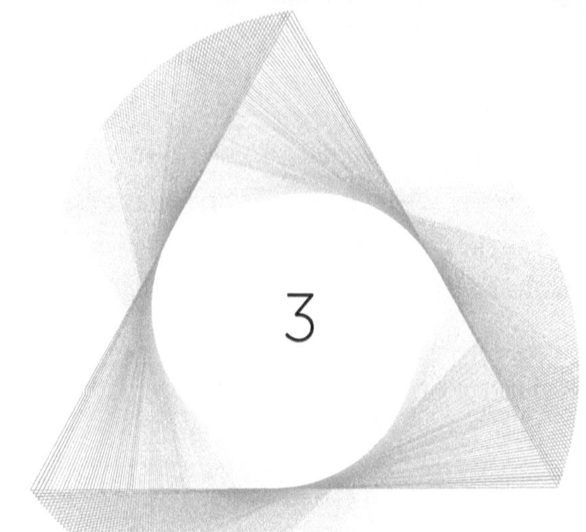

3

The Leader's Journey

Both God's Work *and* Our Faithfulness

God asks for something vivid and strong. He asks us to
cooperate with him, actively willing what he wills,
our only aim his glory.
AMY CARMICHAEL

PICTURE A TANGLED ball of string. It's a mess of knots, some
small and tight, others large and overwhelming. As the one holding the
string, you desperately want to untangle it, straighten out the mess, but
every time you tug on one end—the end you think is the right one—a
different part gets tighter. The problem isn't that you lack willingness
or ability; it's that you lack perspective. You cannot see how one knot
is tied to a dozen others, or which small, hidden knot, if loosened first,
would unravel the entire section.

In the same way, our spiritual lives are complex, and the
"knots" of change we face are often interconnected in ways we

don't understand. If we try to set the change agenda in our own strength, we inevitably pull on the wrong part and make the knots worse.

Spiritual growth requires us to defer to the Master Knower who is also the Master Worker. God alone, who created the string and knows the exact structure of every tangle, provides the knowledge— the correct starting point, the right tension, and the necessary sequence— and the enabling power to set things right. Our role is to listen for his instruction through Scripture, prayer, and the counsel of trusted voices, then exert the specific, faithful effort he directs us to.

This dynamic is key: We relinquish the right to decide which knot to untangle and focus instead on the single task he has prescribed. True spiritual growth is not an either/or process— it's both/and. It demands *both* the humility to depend on God's superior power and wisdom *and* the faithfulness to do the specific things he illuminates. Our work is an obedient response to his direction, empowered by his Spirit. We address one challenge at a time, trusting God to guide our hands. A cooperative dynamic between God and each of us—his work in full harmony with our faithfulness—is a foundational principle we must understand if we hope to lead others in the way of Jesus. This raises a crucial question: What is the central task that God holds us responsible for?

The Leader's Core Responsibility: Abiding in Christ

The answer is simple yet profound:

"Martha, Martha," Jesus said with compassion to his friend in Luke 10:41–42. "You are worried and upset about many things, but few things are needed—or indeed only one. Mary has chosen what is better, and it will not be taken away from her."

What exactly was Mary's better choice? It was simply to forgo other activities and sit at the feet of Jesus. This act of devotion was recorded in Scripture and has since influenced tens of millions of people. Her life of devotion has become a powerful example that has led many! Similarly for us, there is a vital connection between authentic spiritual influence and our willingness to linger before Jesus. Abiding in him is the core responsibility the Lord has delegated directly to us for spiritual growth.

Jesus made this truth abundantly clear. In John 15, he describes himself as the Vine and us as the branches. Our ability to bear spiritual fruit comes only through a consistent and conscious choice to open up our hearts and receive from him.

> No branch can bear fruit by itself; it must remain in the vine. Neither can you bear fruit unless you remain in me. I am the vine; you are the branches. If you remain in me and I in you, you will bear much fruit; apart from me you can do nothing.
>
> JOHN 15:4–5

A branch's fruitfulness is entirely a matter of its connectedness to the Vine. The primary fruit in our lives is Christlike character which cascades into spiritual impact on those around us. The power to grow is solely the Vine's. Yet the branch must *choose* to remain. This is the both/and reality of abiding—God's constant supply and our faithful receiving. The extent to which we receive through abiding, then, is directly related to the level of fruit we are able to bear. A tender shoot may produce a grape or two, but it's the branch that has developed a mature girth—the strength of deeply formed character—that can bear fruit sustainably without snapping off!

God pays such close attention to the development of our inner lives because he wants to bless and work through us in increasing ways. Paul reminds Timothy that "in a large house there are articles not only of gold and silver, but also of wood and clay; some are for special purposes and some for common use. Those who cleanse themselves from the latter will be instruments for special purposes, made holy, useful to the Master and prepared to do any good work" (2 Timothy 2:20–21). God doesn't want us to break under the pressure of new responsibility. He knows we require thicker fiber—stronger character and new aptitudes—before we can bear more weight. Thankfully, he's made it possible for us to grow into our potential through choosing to develop a sturdier, life-giving connection to the Vine. This is a perfect picture of the both/and of our effort and God's enablement. How amazing that the Creator of the universe desires both intimacy and partnership with us and works within us to make it possible!

Only by the Spirit

This incredible partnership—where God works within us to make growth possible—is accomplished only through the Holy Spirit. The Spirit's life-giving power is fully experienced as we actively draw near to him. Paul assures the Philippians, "Being confident of this, that he who began a good work in you will carry it on to completion until the day of Christ Jesus" (Philippians 1:6). He speaks a similar promise to the Thessalonians: "May God himself, the God of peace, sanctify you through and through. May your whole spirit, soul and body be kept blameless at the coming of our Lord Jesus Christ. The one who calls you is faithful, and he will do it" (1 Thessalonians 5:23–24). God isn't like a distracted renovator who starts a project and then gets bored. He stays committed and finishes what he set out to do.

We must accept that spiritual growth isn't a do-it-yourself project. It's a supernatural process through and through. This truth is foundational: The Christlike character essential for leadership cannot be developed by human effort alone. Sinful human beings cannot change themselves on a spiritual level any more than a lamp unplugged from the wall can turn itself on. In the words of Hannah, who miraculously became a mother and gave birth to the prophet Samuel, "It is not by strength that one prevails" (1 Samuel 2:9).

Spiritual life begins by the will of God and continues through his power. Ephesians 2:1 teaches that before we knew Jesus, each of us was dead in our sin and transgression. We were not just barely surviving on life support; we were wholly deceased, with all the spiritual capacities of a rotten corpse! We are only spiritually alive now because God has given us the Holy Spirit. How silly would it then be if we attempted to grow, lead, or serve without conscious dependence on that same Spirit?

We don't earn or accumulate spiritual life and power through good deeds. All the knowledge and learning in the world also won't cut it. Performative rituals on their own accomplish nothing. This is something which can be hard for religious people to understand, which is why the Pharisee Nicodemus needed Jesus to tell it to him straight. Knowing God begins with something humanly impossible: being spiritually reborn (John 3:5).

Authentic character change happens through this same life-giving mechanism: the power of the Holy Spirit. Despite knowing we are initially saved this way, Christians quickly gravitate back toward human-centered strategies for spiritual growth. Paul didn't mince words with the backsliding Galatian church: "Are you so foolish? After beginning by means of the Spirit, are you now trying to finish by means of the flesh?" (Galatians 3:3).

Apparently, this is an ancient problem.

This side of heaven, even truly converted people retain a sin nature. We remain prone to resist God's presence and direction in our lives. We are slow to trust him and try to take back control wherever we can. But God has given each of us a new spiritual nature able to overcome the old. The Holy Spirit creates holy and good desires where there used to be only sin and selfishness. He then empowers us to live out our new nature each day. As South African writer Andrew Murray explains,

> God works to will, and He is ready to work to do, but, alas! Many Christians misunderstand this. They think because they have the will, it is enough, and that now they are able to do. This is not so. The new will is a permanent gift, an attribute of the new nature. The power to do is not a permanent gift, but must be each moment received from the Holy Spirit. It is the [person] who is conscious of [their] own impotence as a believer who will learn that by the Holy Spirit [they] can live a holy life.[1]

Trying to grow and serve God through your own power quickly becomes an awful experience. I don't recommend you try! Corrie ten Boom, who survived a Nazi concentration camp, knew a thing or two about staying faithful under pressure. She says, "Trying to do the Lord's work in your own strength is the most confusing, exhausting, and tedious of all work. But when you are filled with the Holy Spirit, then the ministry of Jesus just flows out of you."[2]

Christlike character development is therefore markedly different from worldly self-improvement. While physical discipline and therapeutic strategies are valuable, they're limited. You may feel this is an overstatement, as self-improvement efforts often seem to accomplish a great deal. People do overcome adversity and dysfunction to become better versions of themselves. But what's the difference between becoming a "better person" and becoming a "new person"?

Whereas self-improvement polishes the personality, growth that comes through the Spirit transforms the soul. A well-rounded biblical worldview should save us from surprise that certain psychological strategies are effective in bringing about real change. At its best, social science simply observes the cause-and-effect processes in the real world—a world God created and ordered. When researchers discover, for example, that drug addicts are more likely to succeed with a support group, they are simply proving and expanding on the biblical truth that we are relational beings made in God's image. Humans flourish and excel in community. We suffer and dwindle in autonomy. This is true for all of us, whether Jesus is part of the picture or not.

Many secular resources teach invaluable skills transferable to Christian service. For instance, in my undergraduate studies, a mentor introduced me to Dale Carnegie's business literature classic *How to Win Friends and Influence People*. Carnegie's book offers social tips and tricks that could apply to any sphere of human relations, such as demonstrating sincere interest in others and remembering significant details about their lives. These are key skills for every Christian as a called ambassador for Christ (2 Corinthians 5:20). The world has enough Christians who are weird in all the wrong ways. But behavioral adjustments aren't the same thing as fundamental or deep change. That has to happen on a heart level. Dale Carnegie's book may teach me how to make another person feel appreciated, but learning his techniques doesn't make me a truly loving person; it only teaches me to act like one.

Growth that comes through the Spirit looks different. It also often happens in times or in ways that may surprise us. God, for instance, might use circumstances to reveal to us a sin problem that was previously obscured. Even as we serve him, he allows us to struggle in areas of natural strength so we might learn humility and dependence, rather than thinking we need him only in the places we are obviously weak. Often, like novice math students, we don't understand the order of operations, but the sequence is not our concern. God in his sovereignty oversees our growth and determines its pace. He's the ultimate project manager. This patient step-by-step process is not about a quick fix or a simple makeover; it's about a complete, fundamental change.

God isn't like one of those cheesy hosts on HGTV remodeling shows we have in the United States. They're hunting for cosmetically deplorable homes for a quick renovation and resale. The Holy Spirit is about utter transformation. In *Mere Christianity*, C. S. Lewis puts the principle in brilliant metaphor by comparing God's redemptive work in us to a horse being remade into a Pegasus. He points out that this transformation is about creating a powerful and entirely new creature, rather than simply a marginally improved horse.[3] This is a true sort of alchemy in which God takes the ordinary and makes it extraordinary. Authentic Christian leaders live lives that can't be explained away as just the product of hard work and a good upbringing. It must be apparent that by God's grace we are becoming something new entirely.

Not Without Us

We've established that character change is God's work, but the Bible clearly teaches we still have a part to play. It's a both/and reality—the cooperative dynamic we identified at the start of the chapter. God is fully at work, yet we have a crucial role. Philippians 2:12–13 places these twin truths side by side: "Continue to work out your salvation with fear and trembling, for it is God who works in you to will and to act in order to fulfill his good purpose."

Unless we think Paul is openly contradicting himself, we have to believe that both these statements are somehow true. Our role isn't about earning salvation, but about actively participating in the process God has started. Any view of spiritual growth that leaves out our responsibility is incomplete. The fact that human choices matter to spiritual development is apparent in how the Bible calls us to action. Ephesians 6:10–11 urges us to "be strong in the Lord …. Put on the full armor of God, so that you can stand against the devil's schemes."

The spiritual armory is fully stocked, but it won't do anything unless we put it on. Shields don't automatically block arrows. They must be raised. Swords won't parry on their own accord. The consequence of inaction is clear: We leave ourselves wide open to Satan's schemes.

The Holy Spirit grows each person according to God's unique plan. But some conditions are more favorable to growth than others. A fern with enough water and nutritious soil will flourish. A neglected plant withers. The same dynamic is true for us. Earnest prayer and meditating on Scripture aren't automatic; they must be chosen day by day. It is up to us to search out and facilitate the conditions God recommends, and then trust in him to do what we cannot: generate the growth.

How can we explain why some believers grow so much more than others in the same amount of time? Why are some leaders much more qualitatively fruitful than others? We know there is no inequality in God's love, acceptance, or any other fundamental spiritual blessing listed in Ephesians 1:3–14. Those gifts are inherent to being in Christ. Surely, we worship a God who loves all people and gives them all they need for spiritual fulfillment.

There is only one answer: It matters greatly what we choose to do with all that God gives.

When teaching Timothy about spiritual leadership, Paul urged, "Be diligent in these matters [referring to Timothy's own speech and conduct]; give yourself wholly to them, so that everyone may see your progress. Watch your life and doctrine closely. Persevere in them, because if you do, you will save both yourself and your hearers" (1 Timothy 4:15–16).

Notice the vital connection: Persevering in your own growth is the criterion for participating in saving others. In this context, "save" doesn't mean earning salvation to receive eternal life but refers to helping others grow in their faith.[4] Timothy could only help others on their journey of sanctification (becoming more like Jesus) to the extent he himself was willing to invest in his own spiritual growth. As Chinese church planter Watchman Nee observed, "Anyone who serves God will discover sooner or later that the great hindrance to his work is not others but himself."[5] It's tempting to blame-shift when facing failure, but a person of humble character knows the actual hindrance to their work is often internal. This principle applies to all leaders: Our ability to influence others for Christ is directly tied to our willingness to grow in Christlikeness ourselves.

How We Cooperate: Four Choices

I could fill a hundred pages with Bible verses outlining everything that human cooperation with God entails. But there are some things we know for certain that God has sovereignly placed within our control. Consider the following choices:

- **Listen:** No one can learn without first listening. Listening is a choice to focus our minds and be attentive to what the Lord is saying. Listening plays out in how we pray, the way we receive the wisdom of others, and our attitude when studying God's Word (Proverbs 2:1–5, Proverbs 19:20, Matthew 4:4, Mark 4:24, Luke 11:28, Romans 10:17, James 1:19, Hebrews 3:15, Revelation 3:20–22).

- **Seek:** God readily makes himself available to those who seek him. We're not just sitting back and waiting to be changed by God; we're actively looking for what comes next (1 Chronicles 16:11, Proverbs 8:17, Psalm 34:10, Isaiah 55:6–7, Jeremiah 29:13, Lamentations 3:25, Matthew 6:33, Matthew 7:7–8, Acts 17:26–27, James 1:5, James 4:8).

- **Believe:** Believing is an exercise of faith. While God reveals his promises, we have to choose to believe them.

God often uses circumstances to bring us to crossroads of faith where untested spiritual knowledge becomes insufficient. Faith is the decision to rest real weight on the promises of God. How we live demonstrates what we actually believe is true (Genesis 15:6, Proverbs 3:5, Psalm 37:4–6, Mark 5:36, John 14:1, Acts 16:31, Romans 10:9, Romans 15:13, Hebrews 11:1–6).

- **Yield:** Our sinful nature wants to flee from God's presence. It requires an act of will to stay and allow God to work in our lives. God is the Great Physician, healing and operating like a surgeon on human hearts, but we have to stay on the operating table! (Psalm 119:32, Psalm 139:7–10, Jonah 1:3, 2 Timothy 1:7, Hebrews 3:15).

The Joy of Partnership

In his novel *The Voyage of the Dawn Treader*, C. S. Lewis illustrates how spiritual growth is a product of *both* God's work *and* our cooperation. Eustace Scrubb is a spoiled boy who transforms into a dragon as an outward manifestation of his inner greed and selfishness. Although he initially enjoys his newfound power, before long he realizes it would be better to be a boy again. He soon despises his scaly skin and tries to scrape it off, but he is powerless. Finally, the great lion Aslan appears and offers to remove Eustace's scales. Swallowing his fear, the dragon-boy allows Aslan to dig in his claws and painfully peel back the dragon flesh until Eustace is a boy once more. Like Eustace, we can't deal with our sinful nature on our own. But God can! However, we do have to understand our part, and allow him go to work.[6]

It would be great if we automatically knew what it would take to see real change in our lives. But truth be told, if we had eagle-eye vision and saw the full road ahead, we'd probably be tempted to bail! This is why it's wise to focus on taking the steps God puts right in front of us. We don't need the full map; we just need to patiently work the "knot" he reveals to us. As C. S. Lewis observes in *The Screwtape Letters,* Satan often tries to draw us out of what God is presently doing into the realm of speculation and fantasy about the future. The devil wants us anxiously fiddling with what might be, relishing our attempts to control what is unknown and has not been revealed, because the future is the most temporal and uncertain part of time. God, on the other hand, wants us to attend to the present, where we can experience peace through his promises and come to him daily for the strength and guidance we need.[7]

A perceived tension between God's sovereignty and human responsibility can paralyze some people with confusion and doubt. But a biblical understanding of our appointed role in spiritual growth ought to grant us great assurance. We are not left to figure this out on our own, nor are we passive spectators. Instead, we are invited into a divine-human partnership where God's power meets our faithfulness—a synergy essential to Christlike character development. When we embrace our role in this process, we can step forward with confidence, knowing that God is faithful to complete the good work he began in us.

Understanding how character change works is helpful. But it's the blessings that come with it that ought to really get us excited. God isn't just in the business of breaking us down—he is also in the business of building us up.

He loves to give us better things than we would have chosen for ourselves. As we grow in Christlikeness, we experience the joy of becoming the people God created us to be. And as our character is transformed, we are equipped to lead others—not from a place of striving or self-reliance, but from the overflow of God's work in us. It's an amazing experience we should want not only for ourselves, but for every person! This is the heart of a life that leads: faithful service that flows from a life shaped by God's grace and power.

PART TWO

PRACTICING A LIFE THAT LEADS

In part one, we approached the concept of Christlikeness much like a painter begins with a new canvas. We started with the broad brushstrokes, defining the essential shape and composition of the leaders' life and the ultimate goal of our faith. But a painting is more than just an outline. It needs life. It needs color, texture, and light to move from a sketch to a masterpiece.

Now, in part two, we'll begin that more detailed, practical work. We'll delve into some of the specific attributes that form a leader's Christlike character and consider how these translate into the visible and tangible aspects of a leader's life.

The traits we'll explore are mostly drawn from the apostle Paul's Pastoral Epistles to Timothy and Titus. Paul wrote these letters to guide the next generation of Christian leaders, instructing them not just on what to do but on who to be—a life that leads according to Christ's example.

The qualities selected are not an exhaustive list, but they serve to illustrate the relationship between growth in character and the spiritual impact we have on others. For each trait, we'll explore what it means in biblical terms and how it ought to play out in the life of a leader. This also means naming the specific struggles and pressures we may face in living it out, and what's at stake if we don't. We will then examine Jesus' model and provide concrete practices for applying his example in our everyday life and leadership. (See appendix one for the broader argument that these qualities form a total picture of Christian maturity which applies to all believers, regardless of cultural context or level of leadership in the church.)

The following traits will be our focus in the chapters ahead:

- *Not self-willed*—a core element of Christlikeness, where a leader's surrender to God lays the groundwork for all subsequent growth.

- *Holding firm to God's Word*—a personal, active engagement with Scripture that provides the wisdom and discernment a leader needs.

- *Sensible,* or full of sound judgment—the natural outcome of a surrendered heart and a mind saturated with God's Word.

- *Manages own household well*—the journey begins at home, where a leader's spiritual influence is first tested and proven in their most intimate relationships.

- *Eager to serve*—a joyful, active expression of faith, fueled by eagerness to see God at work.

- *Hospitable*—bridging the gap between the familiar and the external, demonstrating a leader's active love for strangers and an outward focus on the church's mission.

- *Gentle*—vital for engaging with the wider world, expressing a leader's emotional maturity and wisdom to deal with people's weaknesses in a non-rigid way.

- *Able to teach*—the practical skill of making personal knowledge transferable to others, ensuring a leader's private growth becomes a public source of edification.

- *Not double-tongued*—consistent and honest communication, demonstrating reliability and building trust by avoiding shallow promises and impossible commitments.

- *Just*—a key outward expression of character, demonstrating a commitment to what is right, no matter the cost.

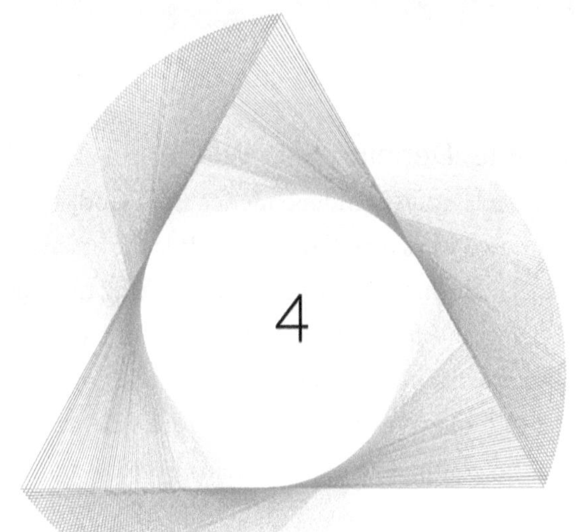

4

Surrendering to God and Others

"Not Self-Willed"

For the overseer must be beyond reproach as God's steward, *not self-willed*, not quick-tempered, not overindulging in wine, not a bully, not greedy for money.

TITUS 1:7, NASB

IF YOU'VE EVER seen a toddler throw a tantrum because they couldn't have their own way, you've witnessed pure self-will. As adults, we learn to disguise our resistance, but it doesn't disappear; our tantrums simply become more mature and subtle. The core issue remains: a stubborn refusal to be corrected or limited. This is the spirit of self-will that the apostle Paul warns against in leaders.

The Principle: Defining Self-Will

Self-will is a declaration of independence from God, a proud insistence on our own ways over God's ways. It is the essence of Adam and Eve's original sin. God gave them everything they needed for their well-being and flourishing. But instead of trusting in God's wisdom and provision, they chose to follow their own desires and judgment. Modern expressions of self-will are a direct echo of their original sin and continue to block humans from the transformative grace of God.

At its heart, self-will is a form of self-idolatry—a refusal to let go of our perceived control and a demand to have reality conform to our own image. Jeremiah described the Exodus era of the Israelites in these terms: "But they did not listen or pay attention; instead, they followed the stubborn inclinations of their evil hearts. They went backward and not forward" (Jeremiah 7:24).

The Struggle: Resisting Surrender

Why is it so hard to surrender our will to God and others? Self-will is a treacherous enemy of spiritual growth because of its ability to camouflage. Self-will can look like the bold and offensive defiance of the person who always demands their way, or it can be the more secretive form of the autonomous person who doesn't share their plans in order to avoid criticism. Self-will can look like outright rejection of God's will, but it can also manifest as a self-righteous attitude or a self-centered approach to leadership.

The self-willed person fails the crucial test of leadership by refusing to learn from their mistakes. It shouldn't require great force for Christians to accept an error and change direction. "Do not be like the horse or the mule, which have no understanding but must be controlled by bit and bridle or they will not come to you" (Psalm 32:9).

Watchman Nee laments,

> Unteachability is one of the most tragic aspects of [self-will]. If a person cannot learn, what possibility of advance is there? If we can be thoroughly delivered from our reluctance to accept instruction, so that we receive it without hesitation, we shall be able to move on swiftly from one new lesson to another. There are endless lessons to be learned in the spiritual realm, so we must be prepared to receive help from many quarters. Unless we become better learners we shall make pathetically little progress even in a lifetime.[1]

What happens when we won't let God break us of stubborn self-will? Any ministry built through self-will falls apart over time. People lose respect for someone clearly acting out of pride and insecurity or who needs to have their own way. Real fruit in ministry comes not through self-effort but by abiding in Christ. Before long, the hollowness of self-willed leadership soon becomes apparent.

Self-will leads to poor discernment and bad decisions in Christian ministry. Self-willed people tend to measure opportunities by their own ambitions and abilities, rather than God's plan and resources. This often results in choosing the wrong investments for the wrong reasons. It leads to sticking with a misguided plan longer than they should, simply because it was their idea.

Self-willed leaders ironically limit themselves by either trying to force their way of doing things or retreating into what feels controllable. In both instances they tragically cut themselves off from God's provision. There is a diversity of spiritual gifts in the body of Christ for a reason, but this truth escapes the self-willed leader. Without a transformed character, a self-willed leader will inevitably face one of two outcomes: isolation or an echo chamber of "yes-men." Both are disastrous for the leader and those they serve.

Self-will can be evidenced by a lack of prayer or consistently attempting ministry in the power of the flesh. Self-willed leaders find it distasteful to take input from others. But avoiding wise counsel places them in the category of fools. "The way of fools seems right to them, but the wise listen to advice" (Proverbs 12:15).

Jesus' Example: Perfect Submission

Jesus modeled perfect submission to the Father's will, the very opposite of self-will. His life was a testament to the principle that true strength comes from surrender. In the Garden of Gethsemane, in the face of unimaginable suffering, he prayed, "My Father, if it is possible, may this cup be taken from me. Yet not as I will, but as you will" (Matthew 26:39).

Jesus bowed to the Father's plan, showing that true victory is found in obedience, not autonomy. When we humble ourselves before God, he promises to lift us up in honor (1 Peter 5:6).

The Path: Four Practices for Cultivating a Humble Heart

What can growing leaders do to escape self-will?

- **The Practice of Self-Reflection:** Prayerfully reflect on the roots of autonomous self-reliance. Ask yourself: *Why do I respond so sharply to constructive feedback?* Some of us may have felt we had to fight for respect and safety as children. Self-willed behavior can in some instances be a learned self-protective strategy for survival. Taking the time to unearth old wounds and deal with them in the light of God's grace has the potential to be transformative. Sometimes we may even need to forgo a ministry project until we've taken the time to receive help through good biblical counseling.

Next Step: Try setting aside a few minutes each day or each week to journal about your reactions to feedback or disagreement with others. Consider how past hurts could be influencing your responses.

- **The Practice of Embracing Teamwork:** A central part of spiritual leadership is being able to work well with others. Team building is an essential leadership skill. But self-willed people cannot operate effectively in teams. To grow in this area, actively seek opportunities to collaborate, and learn to highly prize the contributions of others. View account-ability and cooperation not as inefficient but as a vital part of God's design for the body of Christ. We should all be able to reference recent times we have deferred to someone else's way of doing things or sought to support someone else's initiative. Next Step: Ask a teammate, friend, or collaborator for an honest assessment of what it's like to work with you on a shared goal or project. Remember that "faithful are the wounds of a friend, but deceitful are the kisses of an enemy" (Proverbs 27:6 NASB). I am deeply grateful for my brave and sharp-witted wife who graciously calls me out the moment I begin bulldozing or dismissing others.

- **The Practice of Humility in Prayer:** Prayer is like uncut bleach. It eats away at the stubborn mold of self-will. The Proverbs use the word "commit" when describing how we ought to bring our plans before God (Proverbs 16:3). This implies coming to God with vulnerability, trust, and a willingness to relinquish control. It is like submitting an assignment to a teacher—the work is finished and completely out of your hands. You simply have to wait for your grade and the teacher's approval. Real prayer requires humility, and humility is the very opposite of self-will. "Humble yourselves before the Lord, and he will lift you up" (James 4:10). This suggests we should be cautious about making our plans and *then* praying that God backs them. Honest prayer instead consistently gives God a blank check and asks for preemptive guidance on what we should do. Some of the most radical direction shifts in my life and ministry were delivered while practicing this sort of open-ended, listening prayer. It's amazing what we hear when we pay careful attention to the Holy Spirit.

Next Step: Schedule a session of prayer where you will truly hand over your desires and direction to God. Aim to hold nothing back. Put every dream, goal, and ambition on the table, and then remove your hands. Make up your mind to listen to what God has to say. Receive Paul's encouragement he gave the Philippians: "In every situation, by prayer and petition, with thanksgiving, present your requests to God. And the peace of God, which transcends all understanding, will guard your hearts and your minds in Christ Jesus" (Philippians 4:6–7).

- **The Practice of Differentiating Wills:** We need to understand the difference between self-will and strong will. It is not unspiritual to argue a case. There is nothing noble about withdrawing in the face of any contrary opinion. This sort of deferring can even represent immoral weakness if done out of fear. Paul urged the Corinthians in the strongest of terms, "Be on your guard; stand firm in the faith; be courageous; be strong" (1 Corinthians 16:13). Important matters deserve strong opinions. We too should cultivate a fighting spirit, but one tempered by respect for others and sealed with reverence for God.

  Next Step: In what areas in life and leadership do you need to do a better job of standing your ground? Try your best to identify these—and ask God for the courage to do what needs to be done.

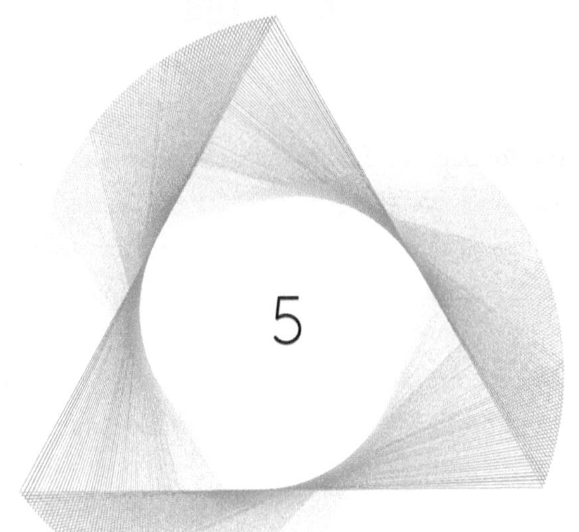

5

Staying Grounded in Scripture

"Holding Firm to God's Word"

Holding firmly the faithful word which is in accordance
with the teaching, so that he will be able both to exhort
in sound doctrine and to refute those who contradict it.

TITUS 1:9, NASB

I ONCE HAD A friend who was struggling with a difficult decision. He was being pulled in different directions by advice from various people, and each sounded convincing. His own biases were also evidently at play. What he needed wasn't another casual suggestion from me, or a personal anecdote, but an anchor—a firm foundation of truth he could rely on. To truly guide him, I had to dig deeper into

God's Word to help him find the clear, unchanging principles that applied to his situation.

Regardless of their role or context, Christian leaders need a growing understanding of God's truth in order to effectively guide and encourage other believers. It takes a strong comprehension of the Bible to correct misunderstandings and confront errors; a surface-level knowledge won't suffice to tackle the complicated problems life tends to throw at us.

The Principle: Learning to Use Scripture Well

Knowing God's Word is fundamental to Christian leadership. Paul urged Timothy, "Do your best to present yourself to God as one approved, a worker who does not need to be ashamed and who correctly handles the word of truth" (2 Timothy 2:15). This is a core responsibility for all leaders—not just to possess knowledge but to handle it correctly. Jesus' rebuke of the Pharisees perfectly illustrates this. He told them they were "in error because [they did] not know the Scriptures or the power of God" (Matthew 22:29). The Pharisees had memorized vast portions of the Old Testament, possessing immense knowledge. However, they failed to correctly handle it. Their knowledge was head-centered, missing its heart and the very God they claimed to serve.

The Bible must be our primary resource because nothing changes people like God's Word. Real spiritual fruit doesn't stem from the mere presence of spiritual gifts. Spiritual fruit comes from the power of the Holy Spirit imparted through God's truth! "And we also thank God continually because, when you received the word of God, which you heard from us, you accepted it not as a human word, but as it actually is, the word of God, which is indeed at work in you who believe" (1 Thessalonians 2:13). Leaders who are transparently in love with God's Word inspire others to delve deep right alongside them. The result is spiritual growth—the very goal of Christian leadership!

The Struggle: Resisting Distraction and Drift

Why is it so hard to remain grounded in God's Word? Spiritual knowledge is a dynamic process that requires ongoing study and application. It's a good start but not sufficient to memorize a few key encouraging verses. Theological drift is a real and present danger for the church. Leaders who once were firm in their beliefs end up subscribing to non-biblical ideologies or wandering into theological error.

A leader without a firm grasp of Scripture is like a ship without an anchor or rudder. In calm waters, the ship may seem fine. But when the storms of life or cultural currents hit, it is easily swept off course, tossed about by every wave, and blown by every wind of doctrine (Ephesians 4:14). A slight deviation from biblical truth is like a compass being off by just a few degrees. Over a long journey, a small error in direction will cause you to miss your destination entirely. Leaders get off track when they lose their biblical moorings. As a result, they sink time and energy into Christian fads while neglecting what's timeless and most important.

Satan sues for heresy and apostasy but will settle for distraction. The current of the world system pulls strongly toward compromise. It's only by continual refocusing on God's truth that the church avoids being totally swept away.

Commenting on the ministry of John Wesley, J. Oswald Sanders observes:

> He never indulged in a cheap disparagement of the intellect and was always trying to promote knowledge of the Scriptures and spiritual renewal among the people. He was intellectually gifted and possessed an impressive command of English literature ....

Yet he was widely known as a person "of one Book." That kind of breadth, focused on the Scriptures, is a high example of the consecrated intellect of the spiritual leader.[1]

Jesus' Example: Perfect Knowledge and Application

Jesus modeled the perfect integration of hearing and obeying God's Word—the principle he calls us to in his Parable of the Wise and Foolish Builders, where he explained that the wise person is one who hears his words and puts them into practice (Matthew 7:24–29). In the wilderness, facing unimaginable temptation, he wielded Scripture as his primary weapon against the enemy, not just by saying "It is written…" (Matthew 4:4) but also by obeying what the Word required—rejecting temptation.

The Path: Four Practices to Stay Grounded in Scripture

Growth in this area often looks like returning to tested and useful disciplines.

- **The Practice of Academic Bible Study:** Academic study moves us beyond surface-level understanding, providing a deeper and more accurate grasp of Scripture's context and meaning. This robust knowledge is crucial for leaders, equipping us to refute opposition, navigate complex issues, and prevent theological drift both in ourselves and those we lead. If time with God has slowly become purely devotional, consider reintroducing academic Bible study to your routine. Challenge yourself. Read difficult portions of Scripture. Engage with hard questions rather than gloss over them. Try cracking open commentaries and concordances or using websites like www.blueletterbible.org. The goal is not just raw knowledge; the goal is to grow in humility, wisdom, and love for both God and others. As we saw in Jesus' example, true growth comes from hearing and obeying as we integrate knowledge and application.

Next Step: Choose a book of the Bible you've never studied in-depth and use a reputable commentary or study Bible to work through it, focusing on historical context, literary style, and key themes.

- **The Practice of Ongoing Learning:** When teaching the Bible, don't just rehash old notes but consider it a new opportunity to learn. God's Word is spiritually dynamic and will lead us to new insights and applications. "For the word of God is alive and active. Sharper than any double-edged sword, it penetrates even to dividing soul and spirit, joints and marrow; it judges the thoughts and attitudes of the heart" (Hebrews 4:12). While God's Word never changes, our personal and cultural context is always in flux. This means some parts of Scripture will speak more powerfully at certain times than at others—finding special relevance in your life, community, or broader society.

  Next Step: Before your next teaching, discipleship session, or small group meeting, pray and ask God for a fresh insight from the passage, even if it's one you've gone over before. Look for a new application or a deeper connection you may have previously missed.

- **The Practice of Seeking Resources for Growth:** Peter directly relates spiritual growth to a believer's hungry pursuit of truth. "Like newborn babies, crave pure spiritual milk [God's Word], so that by it you may grow up in your salvation, now that you have tasted that the Lord is good" (1 Peter 2:2–3). This growth in knowledge is critical because the more we know about God and his will, the more opportunities we will have to exercise faith in a manner that leads to maturity.

Next Step: Choose one of God's attributes and do a topical study. For instance, you could look at every reference to God's "loving-kindness" mentioned in the Old Testament.[2] As you read through these verses and consider their context, ask yourself, *How would it change my life if I really understood and believed these truths?* Combine study with prayer, and ask God to show himself to you anew as you read.

- **The Practice of Imparting Truth to Others:** Leaders who don't know Scripture typically lean on their own charisma to persuade. But this approach won't produce long-term disciples. The true test of discipleship is what happens when the disciple-maker is no longer there. We need to equip men and women with a renewable resource of motivation and wisdom that endures and sustains them long after our direct input is gone. If you were hit by a bus tomorrow, what would happen to your ministry? Hopefully, you have equipped your disciples to keep learning and living out God's Word apart from your influence. This will only be the case if we carefully impart a love for Scripture and teach others to study and interpret it for themselves.

  Next Step: If you are mentoring or discipling another believer, make sure they are equipped to study the Bible using the "inductive" method.[3] This method helps them observe, interpret, and apply Scripture, making their spiritual growth self-sustaining. As you commit to this training, take time to pray that the people you lead will fall in love with the Bible and become mature in handling its message.

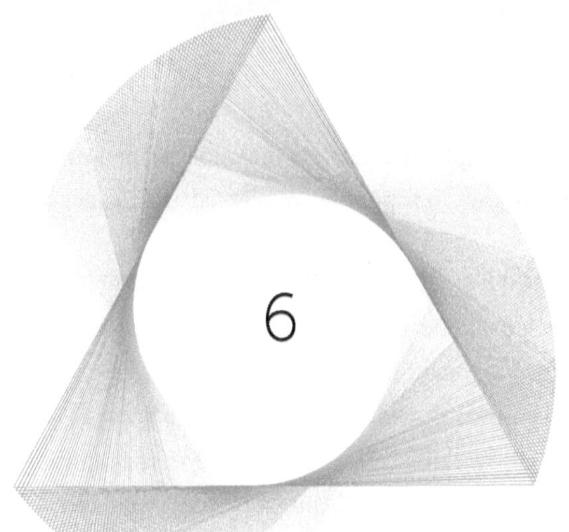

Making Good Decisions

"Sensible"

[The overseer must be] hospitable, loving what is good,
sensible, just, devout, self-controlled.

TITUS 1:8, NASB1995

THE ORIGINAL GREEK word for "sensible" describes someone
who is "in control of oneself, prudent, thoughtful, self-controlled."[1]
Practically speaking, the sensible person is characterized by "careful
consideration for responsible action ... intent on the what, the how,
and the when of doing what should be done."[2]

For ten years, I coached home-group leaders in a large church
network, and over time we saw scores of groups spring up. Some
flourished and are still multiplying. But others have long since
shriveled and died. Reflecting on this, the single most consistent
factor determining longevity and success was sensible leadership.

Engaged and responsive leaders make better decisions than those who aren't—and their people are blessed as a result.

The Principle: The Importance of Sound Judgment

Biblically, sensible leadership isn't just about common sense; it's a state of spiritual readiness characterized by having a clear and sober mind. This mindset, as described in 1 Peter, serves a dual purpose. It's essential for effective prayer and for maintaining vigilance against evil: "The end of all things is near. Therefore be alert and of sober mind so that you may pray.... Be alert and of sober mind. Your enemy the devil prowls around like a roaring lion" (1 Peter 4:7; 5:8). It's a steady hand on the wheel, weighing the pros and cons and ensuring decisions are made with careful consideration. Sensible leaders don't do this alone. They seek outside advice and think through situations as a team.

The Struggle: Making the Right Choices

Sensible leadership is challenging because it requires vigilance, proactivity, and forethought. A leader who is constantly on the back foot—always reacting to problems rather than proactively anticipating them—tends to make poor choices fueled by fear.

Thoughtlessness about the timing of an important event may lead to lower attendance and wasted effort. Failure to anticipate a significant problem can result in major preventable damage. Taking a blatantly disruptive person on a weekend church retreat can pollute the experience for everyone involved, including the disruptor. In contrast, a sensible leader is attentive, sensitive to both danger and opportunity.

Being sensible isn't just about avoiding poor choices; it's also about decisive action. If a leader is consistently slow to make important calls, then missed opportunities start to rack up. Enough misses amount to loss of momentum. Deliberating forever about who ought to step up and mentor a new Christian could mean totally missing your chance to ground them in their faith. Failure to think critically and anticipate what is coming can lead to discouraging setbacks and lost opportunities for growth.

Ultimately, sound judgment becomes more consequential the more people are affected by your decisions. Leaders who fail to grow more sensible over time shift the burden of strategic foresight to their co-leaders, which can become a source of tension and a major barrier to being entrusted with greater leadership responsibility.

Jesus' Example: Perfect Wisdom

Jesus perfectly models sensible leadership by consistently demonstrating self-control, wisdom, and a proactive posture. For instance, when he saw the crowd was hungry, he didn't wait for them to ask for food; he took the initiative to feed the five thousand (John 6:1–14). He also anticipated the needs of his disciples, warning them of persecution to prepare them mentally and spiritually (John 15:20). He often withdrew to pray and seek the Father's will, ensuring his actions were not driven by the demands of the crowd but by God's purposes (Matthew 14:23; Luke 6:12, 9:28). He knew when to speak and when to remain silent, and when to confront and when to walk away.

The Path: Three Practices for Cultivating Sensible Leadership

It's easy to make personality-based excuses for weak character. For example, while being "type-A" might explain my gruff tendencies, temperament should never be used as a justification for sin. Being sensible may not come to you naturally, but fortunately it can be developed spiritually.

- **The Practice of Critical Thinking:** Carving out space for critical thinking is a great place to begin. A sensible leader takes the time to think and pray about those they lead. If you have a hard time tracking key details, get into the habit of jotting down notes you can easily revisit.

  Next Step: Dedicate a thirty-minute block on your calendar this week to prayerfully review your key ministry initiatives or relationships. Ask yourself, *What are the potential blind spots or upcoming challenges here?*

- **The Practice of Learning from Others:** If you can be around people who excel in this area, draft off their experience. What do they focus on? What do they let go of? Although it's important to learn from them, don't become overly dependent on their reads. Instead, develop your own ideas and submit them for constructive criticism. Be willing to be wrong and receive feedback. The best thinking usually happens through honest and open communication in teams.

  Next Step: Identify your current mentors and consider who specifically could help you develop sound judgment. If you don't have a relationship like this, then consider seeking one out. When I was in college, a pastor I knew hosted a weekly fireside gathering, and I prioritized being there, taking every opportunity to pick his brain.

- **The Practice of Studying Proverbs:** Scripture has its own built-in handbook for helping people become wiser. It's called the book of Proverbs—thirty-one chapters of sayings and principles, most of them calibrated to help us make better decisions. Take Proverbs 22:3, for example, which says, "The prudent see danger and take refuge, but the simple keep going and pay the penalty." Or Proverbs 10:19, "Sin is not ended by multiplying words, but the prudent hold their tongues." "Prudent" is a synonym for being sensible. Anyone who spends significant time with these truths from Proverbs will start to form a mental and spiritual lens through which to see the world more clearly and to act accordingly.

Next Step: Comb through the Proverbs and make a list of those you think most apply to leadership and serving God. Choose five, and work to memorize them over the course of the next month.

7

Caring for What Belongs to You

"Manages Own Household Well"

One who **manages** his *own household well*, keeping his
children under control with all dignity.
1 TIMOTHY 3:4, NASB1995

IF YOU'VE EVER had an addition put on your house, you'll know
how important it is to find a good builder. Before the project started,
you probably checked their references, looked at photos of their past
work, and maybe even spoke to former clients. But what if, before you
signed the contract, you decided to visit the builder's own home? What
would you think if you found their roof was leaking, the foundation
was cracked, and the wiring was exposed? No matter how good their
last project looked, you'd likely think twice about hiring them.

This is the same principle Paul applies to leadership. The Bible is clear that spiritual influence must be first seen in our home and in our most intimate relationships. A leader's family life and personal relationships are the true test of their public ministry. The next verse reads, "If anyone does not know how to manage his own family, how can he take care of God's church?" (1 Timothy 3:5). It's easy for a gap to exist between a person's professional and private life. Businesspeople can be attentive and hardworking at the office, but cold and neglectful with their children and spouses. Christian leaders sadly can fall prey to the same dysfunction. They excel in ministry even while failing where it matters most.

The Principle: Establishing Spiritual Credibility

For leaders who are married, caring for their spouse and their children (if they have them), is a fundamental expectation, as it is for every believer. This is because "anyone who does not provide for their relatives, and especially for their own household, has denied the faith and is worse than an unbeliever" (1 Timothy 5:8). A leader whose marriage is perpetually unhealthy will eventually forfeit their credibility. Furthermore, faithfully nurturing our children physically and spiritually is a prerequisite to being entrusted with anything else.

Managing a household well applies to more than just a traditional family. For a single leader, their "household" is their personal life. Discipline and stewardship in this area are a direct reflection of their character. A leader's credibility is inextricably linked to their ability to maintain an orderly personal life, including relationships, finances, time, and living space.

The Struggle: The Gap Between Public and Private Life

Many Christians take on ministry responsibility before they marry or have children. These life-stage changes aren't just exciting;

they can also present precarious seasons of testing. Major transitions bring new temptations and can stir up unresolved emotional baggage. For all leaders—married, single, or in different seasons of life—the struggle is the same: the potential for a dangerous disconnect between public ministry and home life. Navigating these major transitions requires deep humility and an intentional effort to handle changes in a way that fosters spiritual growth and bears lasting fruit, such as a single leader learning to manage their personal finances for the first time, or a married leader learning to say no to a ministry opportunity to prioritize date nights with their spouse.

Ajith Fernando talks about this in *The Family Life of a Christian Leader*:

> Nothing must distract us from building our marriages and families…. God is committed to our marriages and families and will give us all the help we need…. But we must give top priority to our families and dealing with the problems that they face.[1]

Jesus' Example: Perfect Balance

Jesus provides a perfect model of integrated leadership, where his public ministry was an extension of how he managed his own "household" of the disciples. He spent his private time with them—teaching, correcting, and nurturing them. This intimate, consistent care for his "household' was the foundation of the church's future leadership. We also see that he loved his earthly mother and was attentive to her needs, even while dying on the cross (John 19:26–27).

The inclusion of Judas in his inner circle offers us a crucial leadership lesson. Despite Jesus' perfect management and guidance, Judas still chose to betray him, showing us that the standard for leadership is not about guaranteeing the final choices of those we lead but about faithfulness in our role.

The Path: Two Practices for Nurturing Your Household

Success in one season of life doesn't guarantee success in the next. We need to soberly prepare for each stage, as managing our personal life well is a crucial part of our witness, regardless of whether we're single or married. Thankfully, God has given us everything we need. What a blessing it is to navigate relationships—including marriage, parenting, and community life—with others! Although most of us naturally imitate the family dynamics we grew up with, we have the chance to rework our understanding based on the mind of God.

As our society shifts further and further away from biblical views on marriage and family, we will have to fight all the harder to maintain these values. In a world that has forgotten how to build healthy relationships, our imperfect yet thriving marriages, loving families, and vibrant and relationally rich single lives may become our most powerful witness. A wide variety of excellent resources are available on friendship, marriage, and parenting. Read widely and discuss them with others.

- **The Practice of Prioritization:** Remember, God is for our families. Your family is not a distraction from ministry; it's a core component of it. If you are married, no one is better suited to be your ministry partner than your spouse. Similarly, our primary and best disciple-making opportunities may be with our own children. While there are limits to our influence in these relationships, these are still worthy goals to pray on and strive after![2] Leadership in the home means doing all we can to spiritually build up our families. For single leaders, this practice means prioritizing your personal life and well-being, recognizing that your physical and mental health, finances, and relationships are all part of your witness and foundation for ministry.

Next Step: Go over your schedule, and make sure there are clear times set aside to focus on your family. If you are married, this should also mean establishing a regular date night with your spouse. Single leaders with roommates might set up a weekly time to have dinner together and pray.

- **The Practice of Proximity:** While it's important to have protected time alone with our families, we shouldn't overreact and withdraw from Christian fellowship (Hebrews 10:25). At some point, our household is ordered enough. Now it's time to get out and engage the mess of the world around us with the love of Jesus! Christ calls us to live in community. Family life and ministry ought to be integrated in important ways. Having other people over for dinner, hosting times of fellowship, or going out together to serve is good and healthy. Filling our days with such things will give our children a high priority for relationships and serving God. When done together and motivated by God's grace, these activities can become part of a family's identity, forging a lasting, missional legacy that deeply instills the values of hospitality and service in your children.

  Next Step: If you are fully involved in Christian community, then there should be people who have a clear line of sight on your marriage, parenting, and other aspects of how you manage your household. This is a sensitive area of life where it's easy to have blind spots. Choose a wise and trusted person, and ask them for an honest assessment.

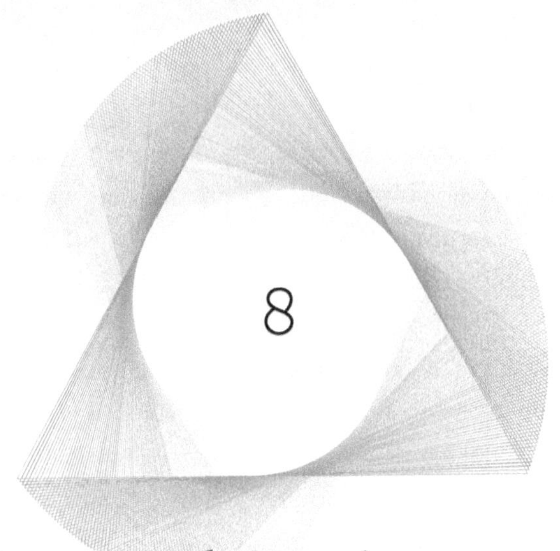

8

Cultivating Consistent Zeal

"Eager to Serve"

Be shepherds of God's flock that is under your care,
watching over them—not because you must, but
because you are willing, as God wants you to be; not
pursuing dishonest gain, but *eager to serve.*

1 PETER 5:2

HAVE YOU EVER known someone so eager to serve that it's almost contagious? Their humility isn't about public gestures but about an earnest, consistent commitment. They're the ones who check in on a person who has been distant, even when no one else notices. They are quick to offer encouragement and slow to take credit, showing up to celebrate a small victory or patiently walk through a season of doubt.

They're the ones who always arrive early to set up and stay late to clean up. Their motivation is not a title or a position but a sincere love for God and others. You get the sense that even if no one else came along, they would still be there, enthusiastic and ready to dive into any opportunity to make a difference.

Jesus ultimately appoints leaders and blesses them with the opportunity to serve. This means that whatever our post may be, it's a gift and not a burden. Paul says, "Since through God's mercy we have this ministry, we do not lose heart" (2 Corinthians 4:1). Therefore, leadership should never be characterized as dreary or purely a matter of duty. Serving in the kingdom of God is joyful and exciting! Now, the privilege of ministry doesn't exclude moments of pain or even whole seasons of frustrating work. But we should try to remain thankful, especially when the work is thankless. Consider how often the apostles found themselves being persecuted, yet they were able to rejoice for the role they were granted in God's great plan (Acts 5:40–41, 16:25).

The Principle: The Heart of Willing Service

Eagerness to serve is a hallmark of mature Christian leadership. While some seasons require us to "tough it out" and do what is right, regardless of our feelings, the goal is to cultivate an inner zeal that reflects the heart of Jesus, who "did not come to be served, but to serve, and to give his life as a ransom for many" (Mark 10:45). This enthusiastic desire to serve others isn't just a personality trait; it's a direct result of our increasing faith in the goodness and power of God.

As we get to know him better—not just know about him—we become more earnest to see his will accomplished. This is what the apostle Paul meant when he said, "I press on to take hold of that for which Christ Jesus took hold of me" (Philippians 3:12). This same drive should characterize our own leadership and be contagious to others. As nineteenth-century preacher Charles Spurgeon once said, "For the sake of our church members, and converted people, we must be energetic, for if we are not zealous, neither will they be."[1]

The Struggle: Resisting Spiritual Decline

The struggle for leaders is our natural tendency toward spiritual decline. Our enthusiasm for ministry can't be dependent on what it feels like, or we will want to give up when we don't see obvious fruit. Enduring leadership needs firm and reaffirmed convictions—the unchanging "why" behind our service. Even the most dedicated leaders can naturally lose their focus over time. Changing circumstances, suffering, and seasons of dryness tend to dim our vision. When this fog sets in and we forget why we are serving, our work begins to lose its flavor.

J. Oswald Sanders comments, "Many who soared like rockets in youth have descended like sticks before the testings of middle life.... There comes a loss of spiritual fervor, a waning of personal devotion, the feeling that we have now earned the right to ease up on self-denial and to indulge ourselves a little."[2] This happens when we get too comfortable and look to settle down. A key sign of waning eagerness is a growing aversion to new opportunities to serve, leading to "play-it-safe" leadership. We find excuses for turning down open doors—whether it's to start a new ministry, take on a different role, or begin a new disciple-making relationship.

Of course, it isn't realistic or spiritual to say yes to everything. But mature faith is always on the lookout to take new ground. The ministry we did years ago doesn't give us a pass on serving now. Tasks that once required us to trust God can become mechanical works of the flesh once we start to feel adequate and in control. We can subtly stop depending on God and begin leaning on our backlog of experiences instead. But taking new, right-now steps of faith keeps us learning, sharp, prayerful, and full of zeal!

Jesus' Example: Perfect Humility

Jesus' entire life was defined by eager service, culminating in the cross, yet one particular action vividly illustrates the principle of humble and eager service: the washing of the disciples' feet (John 13:1–7). This was not driven by duty but a profound, sacrificial love. His actions redefined leadership, showing that true greatness is measured by a willingness to serve selflessly, even in ways that are messy, uncomfortable, or humiliating.

The Path: Three Practices to Develop Eagerness

Eagerness to serve isn't a natural state but a character trait that must be cultivated.

- **The Practice of Seeking Opportunity:** Eager leaders pray with Paul that "God may open a door for our message, so that we may proclaim the mystery of Christ" (Colossians 4:3). We ought to have a bias toward saying yes as often as we can. God will reveal whether it's within his will for us to take on more. But it's on us to adopt the right attitude, expecting God to grow our ministry and living with confidence that open doors are right around the corner.

  Next Step: When did you last allow yourself to be challenged? Pray about whether God may want you to try something new that will require fresh dependence on his power.

- **The Practice of Cultivating Gratitude:** Eagerness to serve is also kept aflame by remaining thankful for what we have. Too often, leaders slowly lose appreciation for their

God-given role. They begin to take God's people for granted. Conscious praise and thanksgiving are basic to keeping our hearts soft. Like old guitar strings, our affections easily get out of tune. Sitting down regularly to thank Jesus for the incredible gift of spiritual leadership is like adjusting the pegs one by one until our hearts sound exactly the way they should.

Next Step: Let God retune your heart through a session of praise and thanks. During this time, name the specific people and venues of service he's placed in your life and recognize them as good and undeserved gifts!

- **The Practice of Maintaining an Eternal Perspective:** We will be eager to serve if we are eager for God. If we believe we are ultimately serving the Creator of the universe, then how can we not be zealous? Jesus said to his disciples, "Truly I tell you, whatever you did for one of the least of these brothers and sisters of mine, you did for me" (Matthew 25:40). We should be motivated by the promise of future reward. As Peter pointed out, "And when the Chief Shepherd appears, you will receive the crown of glory that will never fade away" (1 Peter 5:4). Even the most unpleasant assignment for the kingdom can be received eagerly when we know he sees what we are doing.

  Next Step: Consider a particularly tough situation you are facing. Celebrate that God promises to bless your faithfulness. Remember that even if you never see the earthly result, the Chief Shepherd sees your labor, and your reward will be the unfading crown of glory.

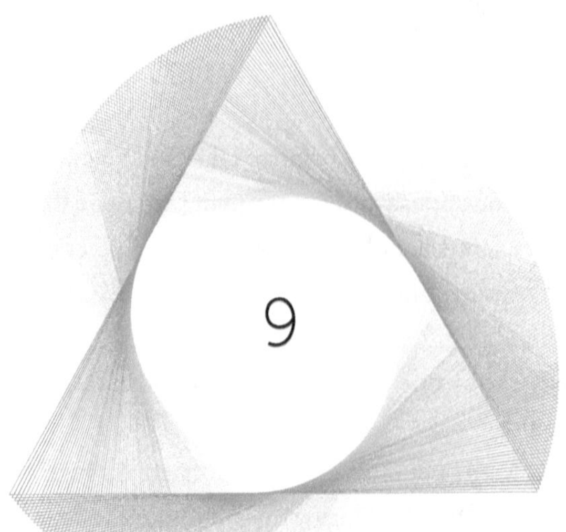

Building a Life of Welcome

"Hospitable"

[The overseer] must be *hospitable*, one who loves
what is good, who is self-controlled, upright,
holy and disciplined.

TITUS 1:8

IT WAS A Thursday afternoon, and I had just finished a long meeting. My mind was reeling from a tough conversation, and all I wanted was to go home and unplug. But as I pulled into my driveway, I noticed a couple other cars were parked at the curb. I'd missed a text from my wife letting me know that some new friends were coming over for dinner and drinks.

My gut reaction was to sulk or shut it down. I was tired, and all I wanted was some time to myself. It's a moment of decision that many of us face. Do we open our lives, or do we shut the door?

The Principle: Radical Welcome

The Greek word for hospitable is φιλόξενος (*philoxenos*) and literally means to "love the stranger."[1] This is a bit different from our English word, which seems to merely describe a place that is tidy and maybe serves good food. This is love that moves beyond our immediate circle of friends and family to those we don't know well. As Paul prays for the Thessalonians, "May the Lord make your love increase and overflow for each other and for everyone else, just as ours does for you" (1 Thessalonians 3:12).

It's easy to enjoy people with whom we naturally connect, but Paul challenges us to let our love overflow to every person we come across. At minimum, this looks like intentionally building a lifestyle of opening our lives and sharing our faith with new people. Effective leaders need to grow in this way of life to keep the church community from becoming inward-focused. Peter connects this practice directly to love, stating, "Above all, love each other deeply, because love covers over a multitude of sins. Offer hospitality to one another without grumbling" (1 Peter 4:8–9).

The Struggle: Challenging the Comfort Zone

Our natural inclination is often to protect our comfort and privacy. As a result, our church communities can easily become inward-focused, appearing loving to those already involved but becoming self-protective and selfish. In these communities, the focus is on maintaining the status quo and keeping existing members comfortable. The body of Christ can feel less like a dynamic, open family and more like a club where members pay their dues for a controlled and curated experience.

This self-protective mindset isn't beneficial even to existing members. It's good for us to be challenged and stretched by new relationships, even while we maintain close friendships. Inward groups often become plagued by disputes and petty dramas that eventually rip the community apart. As leaders, we need to keep our hearts limber, growing, and poised to love new people in new ways. This approach is essential for reaching new people, as evangelism is rooted in relationships. Before anyone can be discipled or mentored, they must first be befriended.

As leaders, we have to fight the tendency for our churches and communities to turn inward. While the church is God's family and some inwardness is appropriate and even necessary for safety, this family-like nature, if left unchecked, can prevent the church from accomplishing its mission to reach the lost. One of our key tasks is therefore to initiate and maintain this outward focus while still caring for committed members.

Hospitality can be more challenging in some seasons of life than others. The close-knit community of a college campus is ideal for building close fellowship and learning how to serve. But post-college life and parenthood require a deliberate effort to adapt. Relationships aren't as convenient, and opportunities to meet new people are harder to come by. Once kids come along, connecting with people can be even more challenging and often requires inviting them to your home or making time to meet them where they are at. These challenges can present a steep learning curve for those who aren't already well practiced in hospitality.

It takes time and energy to make your home a place for effective ministry. What makes your home hospitable has less to do with how much space you have available than the attitude you have toward that space. A ten-by-ten townhouse porch can be better for ministry than a five-bedroom villa when occupied by a person with a servant mindset. When we dedicate our homes to God, he faithfully uses what we offer to him.

Jesus' Example: A Messy, Open Community

Jesus envisioned a community and called his disciples to a way of life that was much messier and more exciting than a private club. His own band of disciples was open to lepers, prostitutes, tax collectors, and anyone else who came to them, regardless of their background. His mission was outward-focused, reaching out to those on the margins. For this reason, any true band of Jesus-followers will end up looking a little odd. Left to our own human preferences, we likely would not have chosen each other as friends. But we are brought together by the fact that Jesus has chosen us and filled us with the Spirit.

The Path: Four Practices for Growing in Hospitality

You can be hospitable in many ways: engaging newcomers at meetings, using your home to host events, cooking meals, creating a warm atmosphere to facilitate times of fellowship, or initiating genuine friendships with non-Christians. If you're not sure what this looks like, one of the best ways to learn hospitality is by being around brothers and sisters who already excel. Hang out with other Christians and get a feel for the way they live out these principles.

Here are four simple practices to help you grow in this area.

- **The Practice of Welcoming:** It's important to be welcoming in spirit but also demonstrate affection. Paul's instruction to "greet each other with a holy kiss" (Romans 16:16) was a culturally common sign of friendship and acceptance in first-century Israel. As leaders, we need to find culturally appropriate methods for showing newcomers that they are loved and welcome—whether it be a handshake with a smile, saying you are glad they are there, or by asking a question or two about their lives. Leaders must be discerning in this. I recommend avoiding what we Americans call "bear hugs" and "noogies" or prying into someone's deepest, darkest secrets in the first hour of meeting them. But let's not commit the opposite error and allow a fear of awkwardness to prevent us from earnestly welcoming newcomers.

Next Step: Do an audit of your own body language and tone of voice when engaging a new potential friend. What are you expressing that demonstrates you are pleased to have them present and open to connecting further?

- **The Practice of Sharing:** True hospitality is about sharing your life and space, not about perfection. Try having people over to your house more often. Perhaps that sounds easy enough. But when we open up our homes, we open ourselves up to real risks. We sacrifice our time and possessions for the greater good of serving others. It's worth taking time to count the cost and consciously entrust your space to God before taking the next step in utilizing it to welcome others. **Next Step:** Solicit honest feedback from trusted, hospitable friends about whether your home feels inviting. Use this feedback to consciously prioritize serving people over maintaining immaculate order. For some of us, however, this might mean hearing we need to clean up a bit more and pay attention to basic aesthetics.

- **The Practice of Cultivating a Hospitable Community:** Leaders must nurture a hospitable spirit that inspires the entire community. Remember, the scope of hospitality can look different depending on temperament and spiritual gifts. Not everyone is an awesome cook, but some of us are great at running games or initiating conversations. Some of the most hospitable people I know are adept at convincing others to share their hobbies or enthusiastically adopting the hobbies of others. They use these newfound points of common interest to connect and build a sense of community. In this way, they imitate Paul who became "all things to all people" (1 Corinthians 9:22), to remove any superficial barrier between himself and another, so the gospel might be unhindered.

Next Step: Try picking up a hobby or activity for the purpose of befriending a neighbor, co-worker, or someone else that God has placed in your life.

- **The Practice of Dependence:** Finally, why not go right to the source! No one loves like God, and no man ever had eyes for lost people like Jesus. Pray that God forms in you his heart for people you don't even know! Become like the missionary Hudson Taylor who, when he saw the surging crowds of China, imagined a "Niagara of souls" passing by.[2] Inspired by Taylor's image, but timid as an evangelist, I used to spend my idle time in college classes praying for my classmates. God used these prayers to grow my love and make me bold. Spiritual change often begins through secret discourse with God. At the end of the day, growing in love for all kinds of people comes from a greater understanding of the way God loves. As Watchman Nee says, "'God so loved the world.' His love included all men, and so should ours."[3]

Next Step: Make a list of the people in your life who don't know Jesus and start to pray for them. Also pray that God would increase your love for them and desire to see them come alive spiritually. If you don't know anyone who isn't already a Christian, then consider going to new places with the purpose of making new friends.

Developing Merciful Discernment

"Gentle"

Not given to drunkenness, not violent but *gentle*, not quarrelsome, not a lover of money.

1 TIMOTHY 3:3

A FEW YEARS BACK, my life was rocked by a quick succession of traumatic events. Several people I knew tragically committed suicide, and a close friend's marriage was ripped apart. During all this turmoil, our first daughter was born. That summer, I experienced sleepless nights and intrusive thoughts. I found myself in a hair-trigger emotional state during the daytime. It really seemed like I was losing my mind. Finally, with encouragement from my wife and friends, I decided it was time to get some professional help and signed up for biblical counseling. It soon became clear that for the first time in my life I was wrestling with severe anxiety.

Before this, I sometimes struggled to relate to people dealing with anxiety or depression. I couldn't always grasp their struggles, and my lack of understanding made me rigid and impatient. But my own experience was the catalyst that fundamentally changed me. It taught me something about what it means to be gentle.

The Principle: Flexible and Compassionate Leadership

"Gentle" in English carries the connotation of a humble disposition and a soft tone of voice. But in Greek, the word has a broader meaning: "Not insisting on every right of letter of law or custom, yielding, gentle, kind, courteous, tolerant."[1] The biblically gentle person then is not easily given to black-and-white thinking. They don't deal with people or situations rigidly but are able to work within the context of human sin and weakness. That is what Paul meant by "gentle."

Through my experience that summer, I learned firsthand that people in the midst of turmoil don't need a one-size-fits-all approach or a rigid list of rules. They need empathy, patience, and a compassionate heart that can make allowances for their weaknesses. This experience transformed my ministry, enabling me to better meet people where they are—not as a leader with all the answers but as someone who has felt the same fragility and understands where they are coming from. It has also helped me in connecting with younger generations who face mental health struggles, because I can now approach them with true gentleness, born from a shared vulnerability.

Being a mature Christian leader is about combining strength and courage with biblical gentleness. Spiritual leaders need backbone to face tough situations. We must be strong and courageous. Paul charged Titus to "encourage and rebuke with all authority" (Titus 2:15), meaning leaders are resolute in their convictions and can defend them when necessary. However, this strength must be tempered by a biblical gentleness. As Paul's words in 1 Thessalonians 5:14 ("warn those who are idle and disruptive, encourage the disheartened, help the weak, be patient with everyone") show, there's no single, universal approach. Different situations require different types of loving action. Gentle leaders can assess a person's spiritual state—whether someone is weak, disruptive, disheartened, or idle—and respond with appropriate care.

Leaders are called to be principled fighters, faithfully maintaining biblical standards by holding "firmly to the trustworthy message as it has been taught" so that they "can encourage others by sound doctrine and refute those who oppose it" (Titus 1:9). But leaders also need to be able to see in shades of gray, recognizing exceptions and taking account of abnormal circumstances.

While "best practices" certainly exist in Christian work, they are not rigid rules. Principles need to be applied prayerfully and lovingly. Such is the nature of disciplining love. Pastoral leadership expert Bill Lawrence offers this advice:

> Taking stands does not mean you should be inflexible; the secret to taking stands is knowing what is worth entering tension over and what isn't. Make certain the stand you take is for the benefit of the person's growth in light of the defined and agreed upon vision and goals, not just for policies, your preference or convenience.[2]

Paul says, "Be completely humble and gentle; be patient, bearing with one another in love" (Ephesians 4:2). In part, this is about adjusting our expectations when encountering challenging or unusual cases. Good leaders can recognize messy growth and distinguish a setback from a hardened state of unrepentance.

The Struggle: Resisting Empathy and Vulnerability

We often wrestle with gentleness because it goes against our natural inclinations and requires a depth of empathy we may not possess. When we neglect to cultivate biblical gentleness, we face significant and painful struggles, both for ourselves and those we serve. If we don't grow in gentleness, we're more likely to alienate people going through difficult times and will be ineffective with those emerging from damaged backgrounds. We'll find it difficult to possess the proper empathy for weaknesses dissimilar to our own, which prevents us from adjusting our approach accordingly.

Our lack of understanding and empathy often makes it easier to write off those with authority issues, for example. Individuals like this are often suspicious and unresponsive to leadership, at least in the short term. But a mature leader understands that patient, relational investment can thaw the most stubborn individuals, and a naturally rebellious person might be won over with kindness if given adequate time and space.

Ultimately, we struggle with gentleness because it requires a vulnerability we often resist. That is why we should be grateful when God allows us to encounter suffering, for it expands our horizons and enables us to better identify with the problems faced by others.

Jesus' Example: Perfect Truth and Love

Jesus perfectly exemplified the balance between strength and gentleness. He knew what was true of humanity in general (John 2:25), yet he was also able to meet each person exactly where they were. For example, he met the learned Pharisee Nicodemus with obscure Old Testament imagery and confrontational language (John 3:1–21). Then, only a chapter later, we find him being personable and clear with the Samaritan woman (John 4:1–26). This blend of firmness and sensitivity is always rooted in genuine care, as Jesus reveals in Revelation: "Those whom I love I rebuke and discipline. So be earnest and repent" (Revelation 3:19).

The Path: Three Practices for Cultivating Tailored Gentleness

God reliably brings about circumstances to teach us to be gentle. But we need to receive the lesson.

- **The Practice of Studying Jesus:** Once again, beginning with Jesus is always a good move. As we explored earlier in the stories of Nicodemus and the Samaritan woman, Jesus is the perfect example of a leader who was both strong and gentle, always tailoring his approach to the individual. Examine his interactions with different people groups and in varying situations. For example, with the disciples, how did he handle their lack of understanding, rivalry, and fear? Or, with the tax collectors and "sinners," how did he treat those who were outcasts and rejected by society?
  Next Step: Do a personal study through the Gospel of John and pay close attention to the differences in how Jesus handled each person who came to him. For each episode ask yourself, *Why did Jesus meet this person this way?*

- **The Practice of Developing Discernment:** Knowing what approach to take in different ministry situations involves the biblical idea of discernment. My friend Conrad Hilario describes discernment like this: "Discernment is a close relative to wisdom. At times, the Hebrew word for wisdom (*hokmah*) refers to a technical skill such as stonework or carpentry. At other times, biblical authors use it to describe someone skilled at living. Thus, discerning people possess a deep understanding of the way people work and how they react to certain situations."[3] There are many ways to become a more discerning person who is also full of mercy.[4] But one of the best is to seek out spiritual people who are both perceptive and kind. Ask them to help you think through complex situations. We often simply don't know how to handle certain kinds of people. The only way to learn is either through trial and error or benefiting from the experience of someone else. Wise and humble people will choose the latter option whenever possible!

Next Step: Personal experience can be helpful in understanding others, but it can also become an unhelpful source of bias. Resist the impulse to judge quickly or assume you already know what is going on. Instead, take a step back and establish a "vertical perspective" by reflecting on God's priorities. Now with focus, and a quiet mind, listen deeply to the person and ask them insightful questions.

- **The Practice of Focusing on Tone and Affect:** Being gentle often has less to do with *what* we say than *how* we say it. If people feel listened to and understood, they are often more willing to hear what you have to say. Pursue and cherish any friends who give honest feedback on your tone and body language, especially after difficult conversations. When it comes to persuading people, these aspects of communication go much further than you might think.

  Next Step: Before engaging in your next tough conversation, pray and think about the right approach. Text messaging, for instance, is rarely the right medium to discuss sensitive issues. Favor in-person communication whenever possible, where you are able to sit, smile, look the other person in the eye, and demonstrate active listening.

11

Transferring Truth Effectively

"Able to Teach"

And the Lord's servant must not be quarrelsome but
must be kind to everyone, *able to teach*, not resentful.

2 TIMOTHY 2:24

A WELL IS ONLY useful if its water can be drawn and shared. A leader's private knowledge of the Bible, though personally edifying, is incomplete if it remains purely internal, like water sealed deep below the surface. It isn't enough to simply know what the Bible says. Spiritual maturity means to become more and more like Jesus. Jesus didn't just secretly commune with his Father. He shared God's words with his disciples and equipped them to live out the truth. "Now they know that everything you have given me comes from you. For I gave them the words you gave me and they accepted them" (John 17:7–8). Our personal experience of God must become something that builds up others. As the apostle Paul says, "Knowledge puffs up while love builds up" (1 Corinthians 8:1).

The Principle: Reproducing Discipleship

The ability to teach involves much more than delivering sermons or speaking from a platform in large venues. In Greek, the phrase refers to any type of formal or informal instruction.[1] It therefore makes sense that spiritual leadership on all levels would involve teaching. The pattern of personal discipleship is, after all, to teach others what you have been taught so that they might obey God and in turn teach others (2 Timothy 2:2). It's important to remember we teach others not just with our words but through the way we live our lives, which is why Paul encourages the Corinthian church to follow his example as he follows the example of Christ (1 Corinthians 11:1).[2]

Growing leaders constantly search for ways to make disciples more effectively. If no one is learning and changing, then is anyone really leading? Charles Spurgeon reminds us that true understanding is displayed by clear communication. "When a man does not make me understand what he means, it is because he himself does not know what he means."[3]

J. Oswald Sanders points out that eagerness to share what you are learning is an indicator of spiritual health. Citing Hebrews 5:12–14, he says,

> These Hebrew Christians had lost that zest to teach and were content to receive all they could for their sluggish, overfed souls. They had become spiritually self-absorbed. Teaching others what we have learned is one of the best ways of stimulating our own appetite for the truth of God.[4]

The Struggle: Ministry Stagnation and Neglecting Results

A leader's ability to pass on what they are learning sets the ceiling for their ministry's impact, yet Christian leaders often struggle with this essential quality, leading to stagnation. This loss of momentum can be born from a lack of ambition to improve our disciple-making, which can be a sign of losing heart for the work itself. Making disciples is our core calling as followers of Jesus (Matthew 28:19–20), so we must do all we can to keep the fire of our motivation burning bright!

Added to this, a significant hurdle is a "let go and let God" attitude sometimes adopted by long-term Christian workers. While this may pose as piety, it is in reality presumptuous and neglectful of our human responsibility for excellent work. Remember the both/and principle from chapter three—God is at work, but he moves in concert with our faithfulness. Since God has given us an actual mission to accomplish, we must care about outcomes. There is a direct link between the attention we pay to our teaching and our concern for real-world results in discipleship. The quality of our teaching is one such area where quantifiable progress could make a real difference. Paul urged Timothy to "keep a close watch ... on your teaching" (1 Timothy 4:16 NLT). Even for those who aren't gifted in preaching, honing communication skills and discipleship methods are still well worth the time.

Jesus' Example: Holistic Teaching for Transformation

Jesus' teaching was defined by effective transfer of truth, resulting in both conviction and belief. This effectiveness stemmed from his commitment to sharing God's words, declaring in his prayer to the Father, "For I gave them [the disciples] the words you gave me and they accepted them" (John 17:8). His instruction was holistic, characterized by authority, clarity, and practical application across diverse settings—from teaching to large crowds (e.g., Sermon on the Mount) to his small circle of disciples privately (e.g., informal, discussion-based instruction). Ultimately, his entire ministry was the model of personal discipleship, instructing his followers not only through words but by showing them what a life surrendered to the Father looked like, so that they, in turn could be sent out to teach and influence others.

The Path: Three Practices to Better Transfer Truth

To keep growing in the proficiency of communicating God's wisdom, try actively pursuing these three practices.

- **The Practice of Discerning Your Strengths:** Discover where you are best suited to teach. Not everyone is meant to teach to large crowds. Some teachers flourish in smaller, discussion-based settings, and others may only ever teach in the context of personal discipling relationships. While we should all be willing to be stretched to try new things, it's also wise to play to your strengths and maximize your gifts. Think of a "big man" in basketball—their strength is dominating the area near the basket, not dribbling on the perimeter. In a similar way, in the body of Christ, our chief concern is to maximize the gifts we do have, and, as leaders, to help others do the same. "Now to each one the manifestation of the Spirit is given for the common good.... All these are the work of one and the same Spirit, and he distributes them to each one, just as he determines" (1 Corinthians 12:7, 11). We should never be ashamed of our gifting or lack thereof. God gives us through the Holy Spirit exactly what he knows we need.

Next Step: With help from a mentor or friend, identify your strengths in teaching and disciple-making. Make sure you are maximizing these in whatever venues you have for communicating God's truth.

- **The Practice of Collaborative Learning:** Very few of us are natural public speakers. Even discussion-based Bible teaching requires some level of training and skill development. Therefore, seek out resources for improving. There is a wealth of online resources on this subject, as well as books and articles. If you teach or preach in a public venue, ask someone with experience to give you feedback. There may even be ways to get help from people outside your community, which can yield special insights. I once traded sermons with a youth pastor from a different church for critical review. Although I didn't incorporate all his feedback, it was eye-opening and beneficial to receive input from someone with an entirely different teaching style than my own.

  Next Step: Before you next teach in any setting, ask at least one mature person to take notes during the meeting and send you clear, actionable feedback for next time.

- **The Practice of Intentional Modeling:** Good teaching is first of all accurate and faithful to what God's Word says. But it also must correspond with the teacher's life and character if it is to be taken seriously. What a leader says will be underscored or undermined by what they do. Authenticity matters more in the long run than ability or gifting. Tim Keller points out, "You may be rather ineloquent, but if you are very godly, there will be a wisdom and insight that is attractive to others.… In other words, your godly character fills in the gaps left by a lack of giftedness."[5] Teachers at any level should take a humble posture and check themselves as to whether they are "practicing what they preach." A teacher's failure to embody a truth they teach creates a dangerous and contagious form of hypocrisy. For this reason, those who teach are held to a stricter judgment by God (James 3:1).

Next Step: Pray David's prayer in Psalm 139:23–24 over your life and ministry: "Search me, God, and know my heart; test me and know my anxious thoughts. See if there is any offensive way in me, and lead me in the way everlasting."

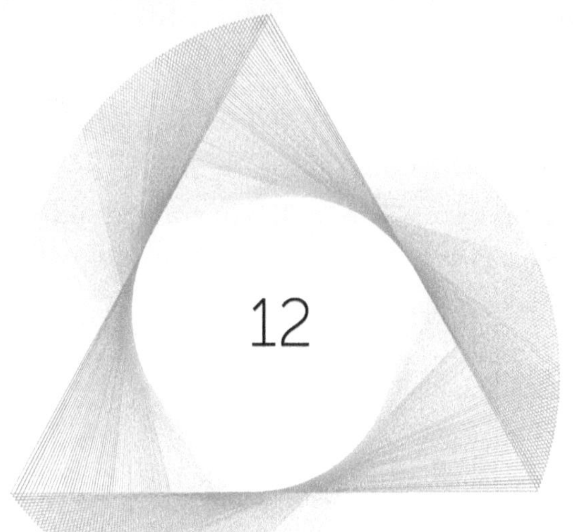

12

Being Honest and Reliable

"Not Double-Tongued"

Deacons likewise must be ... *not double-tongued*, or
addicted to much wine or fond of sordid gain.
1 TIMOTHY 3:8, NASB1995

TRAVIS WAS A seasoned mentor who offered to meet weekly with Dan, a young disciple struggling with anger and consistent Bible reading. Travis committed firmly to meeting every Thursday morning at 7 a.m. to work through Scripture and pray together. Dan rearranged his schedule, viewing Travis's firm assurance as the lifeline he needed. However, after a few weeks, Travis began canceling with vague excuses, and within a month, the meetings stopped entirely with no apology or rescheduling. Travis's double-tongued approach to commitment—saying yes but acting no—broke vital trust and hindered Dan's spiritual growth. This contradiction between Travis's stated commitment and his subsequent actions is precisely what it means to be double-tongued.

The Principle: Honest Reliability

Being double-tongued means being insincere. Like Travis, it's the person who is prone to saying one thing but doing another. This isn't always blatant deceit; sometimes it stems from shallow promises. Fools overestimate themselves, making impossible commitments. Scripture warns against trusting such people. "Putting confidence in an unreliable person in times of trouble is like chewing with a broken tooth or walking on a lame foot" (Proverbs 25:19 NLT).

It's immoral to break promises to God or other human beings: "When you make a promise to God, don't delay in following through, for God takes no pleasure in fools. Keep all the promises you make to him" (Ecclesiastes 5:4 NLT).

Being authentic and exact in speech cultivates trust. The person who eagerly says what they think others want them to say might be a salesman or a sycophant. But they are not a true spiritual leader. Honest and considerate speech should be a defining feature of mature leadership. Intentionally misrepresenting situations by leaving out key information is a form of deceit. Not being forthright about your opinion can also be a form of manipulation. As leaders, we must deal purely in truth for the purpose of love. At minimum, this means being straightforward and factual in how we communicate. We need to remain committed to this principle even when it's costly. As Paul instructs in Ephesians 4:29, "Do not let any unwholesome talk come out of your mouths, but only what is helpful for building others up according to their needs, that it may benefit those who listen."

Christian psychologist Larry Crabb points out, "Words can encourage, discourage, or do nothing. Shallow words accomplish little, death words discourage, and life words encourage. We must learn to speak sincerely with positive impact, using our words to help other Christians pursue the pathway of obedience more zealously."[1]

The Struggle: People Pleasing and Perception Control

We sometimes find it challenging to commit to truth and consistent speech because of a heart-level struggle with people pleasing. Being double-tongued often springs from idolizing the approval of others. We may be tempted to say what we believe people want to hear, rather than the difficult truth, in an effort to maintain popularity or peace.

It can be tempting to charm others with words and through the lure of charisma, but unreliable leaders eventually lose their influence, no matter how charismatic they might be in the moment. People who talk a big game but then don't follow through can't be taken seriously. Over time, they appear fake and untrustworthy. Cynical postmodern culture has a nose for insincerity. People often assume Christian leaders are inauthentic and out for themselves. Double-tongued leaders reward such suspicion. When deceit is deliberate, great damage can be done to the kingdom of God.

Jesus' Example: Perfect Consistency

Jesus' words and actions were perfectly aligned, embodying truth, consistency, and sincerity. He modeled the words he gave to others: "Let your 'Yes' be 'Yes', and your 'No,' 'No" (Matthew 5:37 NKJV). Jesus declared, "I am the way and the truth and the life. No one comes to the Father except through me"

(John 14:6)—demonstrating that he did not just *speak* the truth; he *was* and *is* the truth. Never once in his life did Jesus say or imply something false (1 Peter 2:22).

The Path: Three Practices to Trustworthy Leadership

To cultivate truthful and consistent communication, we need to engage in practices that address the root issues in the heart. After all, "What you say flows from what is in your heart" (Luke 6:45). God desires more than outward conformity. He wants "truth in the innermost being" (Psalm 51:6 NASB). The apostle John knew that real connection with people and God depends on choosing to live fully exposed: "But if we walk in the light, as he is in the light, we have fellowship with one another, and the blood of Jesus, his Son, purifies us from all sin" (1 John 1:5–7).

- **The Practice of a Rock-Solid Prayer Life:** A devoted prayer life that draws both affirmation and direction from God is a great antidote to people-pleasing tendencies. This practice helps us to become secure men and women with developed convictions, so our words and actions closely align. Closeness to God also provides courage. Believing he is truly with us inspires us to follow through and do what is right, no matter the cost (Joshua 1:1–9).

  Next Step: Pick up Bob Sorge's devotional-style book *Dealing with the Rejection and Praise of Man.*[2] Pray over and absorb the challenging principles it contains.

- **The Practice of Transparency:** As leaders, it's important we choose to live fully before God and trusted others, honestly admitting failures, struggles, and limitations, instead of maintaining a perfect façade. Let yourself be seen, even if it means you risk being looked down on or misunderstood. God's grace exists for the person you are, not the person you present yourself to be. Therefore, we should be clear and straightforward in all our dealings, avoiding intentional misrepresentations of ourselves and others.

Next Step: Most of us try to control people's perceptions in subtle ways, sometimes by omitting information or using slight exaggeration. Small moral compromises like these, however, can become footholds for Satan. Ask for God's help to avoid these, and admit to him and others when you mess up. Of course, if you are hiding something significant, you should go and confess it immediately. Only when sin is in the light can you be helped and healed (James 5:16).

- **The Practice of Refusing to Over-Commit:** This involves learning to say no, preventing us from making shallow, impossible commitments. Be clear about what you can realistically offer others, and deliver on it. Often this means taking time to think and seeking advice before you agree to a new opportunity.

  Next Step: When evaluating a new request, don't just check your schedule for raw time; first, ensure you are already being fully faithful to your existing commitments. Once you have said yes, do everything within your power to fulfill that responsibility—not merely to please the person, but out of faithfulness to God.

13

Doing What Is Right

"Just"

[The overseer must be] hospitable, loving what is good,
sensible, *just*, devout, self-controlled.
TITUS 1:8, NASB1995

IN RECENT YEARS, the concept of justice has been at the forefront of global conversations. From calls for social justice in our communities to demands for accountability in corporate and political spheres, there is a widespread recognition that fair and equitable systems are essential for a healthy society. In this cultural moment, it is therefore more important than ever for Christian leaders to understand what it means to be truly just in the biblical sense of the word.

Justice, like all aspects of godly character, must first be worked into the individual human heart, before it can have any hope of affecting the world at large.

The Principle: The Foundation of Righteous Living

The word for "just" in the original Greek refers to a person who is interested in doing the right thing and chooses the good of society over their own advantage.[1] While human perception of fairness is always subjective, justice is bound up in God's very nature. The psalmist affirms this truth, saying, "Righteousness and justice are the foundation of your throne; love and faithfulness go before you" (Psalm 89:14). Because God is just, he desires justice among his people, a theme echoed by the prophet Micah, who declared, "He has shown you, O mortal, what is good. And what does the LORD require of you? To act justly and to love mercy and to walk humbly with your God" (Micah 6:8).

The Struggle: The Temptation to Become Corrupt

Despite this clear biblical requirement, history and current events are filled with examples of leaders, both ancient and modern, who have struggled to live this out. The spiritual leaders of Jeremiah's day were exposed and condemned for their self-centered and unjust practices, with the prophet noting, "From the least to the greatest, all are greedy for gain; prophets and priests alike, all practice deceit" (Jeremiah 6:13). In the New Testament, power-hungry Diotrephes was disciplined by the apostle John because he treated other Christians unjustly, even throwing those who disagreed with him out of the church (3 John 9–10).

A spiritual leader must be sensitive to what is fair and balanced, no matter the nature of their role. Leaders can abuse their position by making key decisions based on what benefits them personally instead of what honors God most. Remaining "above reproach" (Titus 1:6 NASB1995) means being beyond reasonable accusation of corruption. Visible integrity should always be a priority for diligent leaders.

Sadly, no character quality has been so conspicuously absent in many Christian leaders as being just. Scandal after scandal rocks the media as Christian superstar pastors engage in everything from collecting exorbitant salaries and embezzling funds to misusing their God-given gifts for sordid affairs. Often, what once looked like a successful ministry turns out to be rotten at the core once the corruption is exposed. Just as it was with King Saul, the lesson remains clear: God will not sustain even gifted leaders who abuse their positions and prove to be unjust.

Because God is a judge, no injustice will remain hidden. While it might seem like people can get away with corruption and injustice in the short term, everyone will ultimately answer to God. No one will get away with it in the end. Jesus warned, "There is nothing concealed that will not be disclosed, or hidden that will not be made known. What you have said in the dark will be heard in the daylight, and what you have whispered in the ear in the inner rooms will be proclaimed from the roofs" (Luke 12:2–3). Leaders need to remember they are those "who keep watch … as those who must give account" (Hebrews 13:17) and operate with careful integrity.

The larger the leadership role, the greater the temptation to be corrupt. That's why men and women must learn to act justly with lesser responsibilities before being entrusted with anything more. Some qualities can be developed on the job, but justice is not one of them.

Jesus' Example: Perfect Justice

Jesus' ministry was a consistent demonstration of God's righteous character. He interacted with the outcasts and marginalized of society—the tax collectors, women, and the sick—granting them dignity and worth in a culture that oppressed and abused them. He also modeled justice by directly confronting the unjust practices of the religious elite, exposing their hypocrisy and the heavy burdens they placed on the people (Matthew 23). The cross was a pinnacle of divine justice, where God's wrath against sin was perfectly satisfied.

The Path: Two Practices to Grow in Just Leadership

As leaders, we need to be sober about how power can change people. Below are some ways we can cultivate justice.

- **The Practice of Accountability:** Make sure there are always multiple people who have a good line of sight on your life and leadership. Satan loves to destroy leaders since the fallout affects so many people. As our responsibility grows, we must not be naïve about the real danger Satan presents or underestimate the power of our own sin nature. One of the most effective ways to maintain leadership accountability is to always lead on teams. The New Testament leadership paradigm is always plural. None of us are called to be Moses or King David. Embrace team leadership at every level in your ministry or church to ensure thorough systems of checks and balance. For ministries both large and small, this also means maintaining rigorous financial transparency.

  Next Step: Maintaining spiritual peer friendships is vital for personal accountability. Leaders can easily become relationally isolated over time. If you realize you've drifted from people who know you best and are most likely to speak truth into your life, then it is time to reestablish these connections and seek out regular time together.

- **The Practice of Kingdom-First Decision Making:** Unjust leadership can show up even in the smallest spheres of influence. This happens when leaders prioritize their own interests over those they serve. We might call this "ministry greed"—the habit of seeking opportunities that only make *us* look good. Promoting a family member or friend when they lack the necessary qualifications is also sinful partiality. It's good to be ambitious. It's good to believe in our people. But we need to make sure our decisions are based on what's really best for the kingdom, and not our own agendas.

  Next Step: Repent of any competitive spirit in ministry and reorient yourself toward humble cooperation for God's glory alone.

SUSTAINING A LIFE THAT LEADS

14

Soul *and* Skill

The Essential Union of Character and Competence

David shepherded them with integrity of heart; with
skillful hands he led them.

PSALM 78:72

THE MERRIAM-WEBSTER DICTIONARY defines competence
as a "state of having sufficient knowledge, judgment, skill, or strength."[1]
We live in a world driven by hyper-capitalism. Our fast-paced, market-
driven society is utterly obsessed with being competent; results are
everything. Nothing is valued more than the ability to produce—and
not just to produce, but to do it better and faster than everyone else.

The famous US World War II general George S. Patton said,
"Success demands logistical and organizational competence."[2]
Likewise, business and investment mogul Warren Buffett

recommends finding where and how you can be personally competent as the key to being professionally successful.[3] When it comes to the arenas of military and business, good intentions are worthless. It's all about quantifiable impact—the results you can measure.

This raises the question: What role does competence play in Christian service and spiritual growth?

Pastoral leadership expert Larry J. Michael stresses, "The leader today must be committed to ministerial competence. Education, personal charisma, and natural abilities might achieve a short-lived following, but there is no substitute for the continued development of spiritual gifts and practical skills for the work of the ministry."[4]

God Cares About Results

It may surprise some of us to learn that God cares about outcomes and holds his people accountable for their work. 1 Corinthians 4:2 states that "a person who is put in charge as a manager must be faithful" (NLT). In other words, certain roles carry with them real responsibility, and this is as true in spiritual things as it is in any other sphere of life. Anyone given a charge must ultimately answer to the person who appointed them.

Just one chapter earlier, Paul explains the intrinsic connection between the quality of our work (defined as service rendered to God and others) and the spiritual rewards we receive:

> But each one should build with care. For no one can lay any foundation other than the one already laid, which is Jesus Christ. If anyone builds on this foundation using gold, silver, costly stones, wood, hay or straw, their work will be shown for what it is, because the Day will bring it to light. It will be revealed with fire, and the fire will test the quality of each person's work. If what has been built survives, the builder will receive a reward.

> If it is burned up, the builder will suffer loss but yet will be saved—even though only as one escaping through the flames.
>
> 1 CORINTHIANS 3:10–15

Through Paul's analogy, we see that it's more than just the thought that counts. Some people's work will be substandard. While they may still be personally saved, the substance of their efforts in this life can burn up and ultimately count for nothing.

This isn't to say that everyone's service to God is judged the same way. Jesus made it clear that we all receive different abilities, opportunities, and resources. What matters most is what we do with what we have, not how we measure up against others. We are responsible only for the tasks God has specifically laid before us. Consider the Parable of the Talents:

> Again, it will be like a man going on a journey, who called his servants and entrusted his wealth to them. To one he gave five bags of gold, to another two bags, and to another one bag, each according to his ability. Then he went on his journey. The man who had received five bags of gold went at once and put his money to work and gained five bags more. So also, the one with two bags of gold gained two more. But the man who had received one bag went off, dug a hole in the ground and hid his master's money.
>
> MATTHEW 25:14–18

In this parable, every servant who acted wisely and put their funds to productive use was rewarded. Only the servant who did nothing received judgment. Jesus clearly wants his followers to live fruitful lives. As he said, "This is to my father's glory, that you bear much fruit, showing yourselves to be my disciples" (John 15:8). We are aligned with his will whenever we pray for and seek the same kind of fruitfulness.

Leaders are accountable not just for themselves but also for those they oversee. Hebrews 13:17 says leaders "keep watch over you as those who must give an account." My first job out of high school was at Panera Bread, a soup and sandwich chain restaurant here in the United States. One day, my shift manager asked me to go in the back and mix the soups. Typically, this was someone else's job, but it seemed simple enough, so I did it quickly, then moved on to my regular tasks. Several hours and complaints later, we figured out I had accidentally mixed broccoli-cheddar soup with the wild rice soup, costing the restaurant nearly one thousand dollars. I was mortified and prepared for the worst, but instead of getting fired, the general manager apologized to me. It was the shift manager who got written up—he was the leader responsible for ensuring I was trained for the task he assigned.

Because the stakes are so high when it comes to serving God, we must be diligent in our preparation. The apostle Paul uses athletic imagery to illustrate the relationship between performance and preparation in Christian work:

> Do you not know that in a race all the runners run, but only one gets the prize? Run in such a way as to get the prize. Everyone who competes in the games goes into strict training. They do it to get a crown that will not last, but we do it to get a crown that will last forever. Therefore I do not run like someone running aimlessly; I do not fight like a boxer beating the air.
>
> 1 CORINTHIANS 9:24–26

I don't particularly like running, or really any sport for that matter that doesn't involve balls and scoring points. But I grew up in Southeast Asia, where kickboxing is popular, and we would occasionally go to see matches. A boxer throwing kicks and punches in the air may look impressive, but unless he's actually hitting his opponent, nothing is accomplished.

As Christian leaders, we should be even more concerned with the effectiveness of our efforts than professional athletes. How does our training and focus compare with track and field athlete Sydney McLaughlin-Levrone or the late basketball legend Kobe Bryant? Unfortunately, as Jesus once observed, it is often true that "the children of this world are more shrewd in dealing with the world around them than are the children of the light" (Luke 16:8 NLT).

Ajith Fernando, in his book *Discipling in a Multicultural World*, writes, "A biblical leader should be concerned with numbers because the numbers represent people who have come within the sound of the gospel."[5] Undoubtedly, it is easy to become overly focused on numbers. American megachurches have rightly faced criticism in recent years for their business-like prioritization of size over deep, quality disciple-making. While Christians can become so shallow that we discount factors like love, prayer, or real discipleship, the pendulum shouldn't swing so far in the opposite direction that we forget what numbers represent: souls! People are the very reason Christ came and died on the cross. Even now, Peter tells us, God withholds his final judgment because he is patient, "not wanting anyone to perish, but everyone to come to repentance" (2 Peter 3:9). We should serve with the clear goal of increasing the number of people who join the kingdom.

In summary, God cares about results. The degree to which we faithfully accomplish our God-given mission absolutely matters.

Methods Matter

Not long after he was crowned king, David decided to restore the Ark of the Covenant to its rightful place in Jerusalem. Disaster struck, however, when the Levites literally fumbled, and one was struck dead. Later, David rebuked these negligent priests for failing to plan properly and seek God's direction: "It was because you … did not bring it up the first time that the Lord our God broke out in anger against us. We did not inquire of him about how to do it in the prescribed way" (1 Chronicles 15:13).

Methods, it seems, matter to God.

Paul urged his disciple Timothy to "fan into flame the gift of God, which is in you through the laying on of my hands" (2 Timothy 1:6). Timothy possessed great spiritual gifts and was given an important leadership role. Yet talent alone wasn't enough. It was his responsibility to hone those spiritual gifts; he wasn't automatically ready for the job. To fulfill his mandate, he would have to grow and improve as a Bible teacher and spiritual leader.

Faithfulness requires more than just the occasional effort. It demands planning, learning, and being willing to fail, trying again, adapting, learning, and switching approaches when necessary. As Charles Spurgeon said, "If we would win souls, we must act accordingly, and lay ourselves out to that end. Men do not catch fish without intending it, nor save sinners unless they aim at it."[6] Many Christian workers act as though simple, pure devotion is the only thing that matters. This kind of false piety can often mask laziness or fear.

Thankfully, the Holy Spirit compensates for our weaknesses. But his empowerment is for more than just emergency intervention; it is for sustained daily service. He is a constant source of everything we need, helping us grow our competence over time. "For the Spirit God gave us does not make us timid, but gives us power, love and self-discipline" (2 Timothy 1:7). We must aim to do our very best for God while still relying on his resources.

I once visited an older denominational church, where a six-foot-tall placard stood in the lobby. The word "EVANGELISM" was painted in bold letters, and the sign below read: "Tracts handed out: 5,000. Salvations: 0."

Reading it, I wasn't sure whether to laugh or cry. When faced with such pitiful results, faithful Christians should start thinking outside the box. The church was using a tract ministry that had clearly "had its day in the sun." The surrounding post-Christian metropolis—where people don't read much at all, let alone understand the Bible—demanded a different approach. It ought to be the privilege of each Christian generation to prayerfully hone methods that will reach their peers for Christ. It's almost criminal to keep executing traditional systems that long ago stopped making a difference.

Doing God's work well always means doing it his way. We should prioritize strategies that emerge from careful study and fresh, contextual application of New Testament principles. Brian Sanders, founder of the innovative Tampa Underground network of churches, writes,

> Every generation should critique their inherited form, because they are longing for the life of the early church to come again in their time. Every reformation of the church was rooted in this return to a primitive ecclesiology.... It is each generation's responsibility to wrestle with the very customs and traditions in the church that have strayed from the New Testament expression.[7]

Relying too much on tradition is one error, but in practice, churches often move too far in the opposite direction and take their cues from popular culture instead. I agree deeply with Robert Coleman's observation here:

> This is our problem of methodology today. Well-intended ceremonies, programs, organizations, commissions and crusades of human ingenuity are trying valiantly to do a job that only can be done by people in the power of the Holy Spirit.

> This is not to depreciate these noble efforts, for without them the church could not function as she does. Nevertheless, unless the personal mission of the Master is vitally incorporated into the policy and fabric of all these plans, the church cannot function as she should.[8]

Jesus laid down a final pattern for us to follow. Whatever ministry strategies we try to implement, they should always be informed by his example of life-on-life disciple-making.

Leadership Requires Certain Competencies

Hopefully this book has established that spiritual leadership requires people of good character. But specific leadership roles also require specific skills. As Paul says to Timothy, "Do your best to present yourself to God as one approved, a worker who has no need to be ashamed, rightly handling the word of truth" (2 Timothy 2:15). Interpreting Scripture, and helping others understand it, is a core function of spiritual leadership. But this is a skill that must be developed over time, as we explored in chapter five.

LeRoy Eims, who served with The Navigators for fifty years, writes, "Good intentions can't replace good performance. Leaders must be competent in the job God has given them to do."[9] Incompetence can be a grave moral issue. If an incompetent doctor engages in malpractice, it could cost people their physical lives. An incompetent Christian leader may cost people much more.

Sometimes incompetence is the result of simple, honest ignorance that stems from a lack of experience. But there is another type of ignorance that is evil and willful. The fool in Proverbs, despite "a hundred blows" (Proverbs 17:10 NASB1995), still doesn't know what he or she ought to know. At the end of the day, this person's issue isn't a lack of access to wisdom; they just refuse to heed it. "The fear of the LORD is the beginning of knowledge, but fools despise wisdom and instruction" (Proverbs 1:7).

Jeremiah the prophet condemned the so-called spiritual leaders of his day, who were guilty of criminal neglect. They failed to uphold their role as teachers of truth, and the results were disastrous—a whole generation was lost to sin and idolatry. I am sure many of these men were corrupt imposters. But it's likely that at least some were well intentioned but merely spiritually sleepy, too cowardly to take a stand, or distracted by peripheral tasks. Regardless of the motive, the results were the same.

We can see that just as character is foundational, so is competence. Any other conclusion simply falls short of the biblical data. But how exactly do these key areas of growth relate to one another?

The Confluence Principle

Both the Old and New Testaments are littered with examples of gifted leaders who could get others to follow them but could not get themselves to follow God. For example, Diotrephes must have been a man of considerable influence in the Ephesian church. Otherwise, the apostle John would not have needed to publicly confront his corrupt and abusive leadership (3 John 9–10). Saul was an inspirational man of great stature, the first legitimate king of Israel. But he had to be deposed once he proved self-serving and faithless (1 Samuel 15). When God chose David to replace Saul, it was not because of David's superior stature, speaking ability, influence, or charisma (although it does seem like he had a few of these), but because God found in him "a man after my own heart. He will do everything I want him to do" (Acts 13:22).

Character beats skill every time. If we must choose between the two, the decision is obvious. However, we don't need to pit character and competence against each other, as this creates a false dichotomy. In truth, there is a dynamic relationship between authentic character growth and competent leadership.

Think of a leader's ministry as a powerful propeller that drives them forward. This propeller has two perfectly balanced blades: character and competence.

The *character* blade provides balance and stability to the whole system.

The *competence* blade generates the thrust and moves the mission forward.

If a leader focuses only on developing competence (making that blade bigger and heavier) while neglecting their character (allowing that blade to weaken or rot), they create a deadly imbalance. The faster they try to move the ministry forward, the more severe the stress and vibration become, threatening to tear the whole mechanism apart. Great skill is a danger if it isn't matched by character.

Conversely, if a leader focuses almost entirely on developing character (making that blade bigger and heavier), they end up lacking the skills, strategic insights, or organizational abilities needed for the job. The propeller lacks sufficient power to move the ministry forward. The leader may possess immense spiritual virtue, but their work will be characterized by ineffectiveness, missed opportunities, and the inability to execute on God's call. For example, a Christian may have learned excellent self-control through humble submission to God. They may be full of compassion and kindness and possess a dedicated prayer life. But that doesn't automatically mean they know how to disciple effectively. Similarly, teaching and preaching require more than a great devotional life. Training in exposition and delivery is essential. Administrative leadership roles require organizational prowess. It seems therefore that character growth doesn't always result in effective ministry, especially depending on the sphere of service.

The biblical pattern is one of interdependence:

- Growth in character ought to drive increasing competence in the areas a person is called to lead.
- Expanding influence can only be sustained by continued growth in character.

This back-and-forth interdependence is exactly what we see in the counsel Paul gives to Timothy: "Until I come, devote yourself to the public reading of Scripture, to preaching and to teaching…. Be diligent in these matters; give yourself wholly to them, so that everyone may see your progress" (1 Timothy 4:11–16).

Practical Ways to Grow in Competence

To ensure we are not running aimlessly or are like a boxer punching in the air, the internal motivation of strong character must translate into external, measurable progress. Developing the skills needed for leadership involves concrete, intentional effort:

- **Set goals:** Some Christians avoid goal-setting for fear of legalism, yet we set goals for every other area of life where we want to see real results. Someone trying to get fit doesn't typically succeed unless they plan an exercise regimen and structured diet. Likewise, we should not expect to see much progress unless we make actionable plans with clear objectives.
- **Aggressively experiment:** Try your hand at lots of things. We don't discover aptitude through personality tests as much as we do through active experimentation. This is especially crucial for new or young leaders who are still defining their roles and responsibilities.

- **Learn from failure:** Treat every ineffective method or failed project as crucial data. Faithfulness sometimes requires failing. Always take the time to debrief and learn from your mistakes, so they become investments for the future, not just losses.
- **Get in your reps:** Strength conditioning requires the lifter to do many sets over a long period of time. Skill development in ministry follows the same principle. Mastery isn't automatic. If a task is worth doing, do it often, consistently, and focus on improving in increments.
- **Do the study:** Actively seek out the specific resources and insights that will help you excel at the work God has called you to do. This doesn't mean you need to get a master's degree. Depending on the nature of your ministry, that might even be a waste of your time. Instead, read books, take classes, and find learning groups that will help sharpen your specific ministry competency.
- **Lean on others:** We don't have to be good at everything. There are some areas where we simply won't excel, even with great effort. But one important aspect of competent leadership is knowing your limits and learning to delegate to others who possess the necessary strengths.

The Wheel Begins to Turn

I remember the thrill as a young Christian of being able to offer friends spiritual advice and come alongside them in prayer. The more my eyes opened to God's love, the more I desired to be used by him to love others. God was remaking me; I was slowly metamorphizing into a loving person.

But as I sought to love more, I encountered a major problem: For all my zeal, I wasn't very effective. Despite my best efforts and intentions, people didn't always feel the love. In fact, they sometimes ended up offended, hurt, or indifferent.

Seeing this pricked my pride, no doubt. But there was honest pain there, too—I deeply wanted to benefit my friends and family. This gap between intention and outcome made ministry a powerful motivational source for sanctification in my life. I opened my heart to God and asked him to go to work. He began teaching me patience and compassion. I also found myself reading books on how to disciple, teach, listen, and persuade. I applied these techniques, driven by a desire to not only feel love for people but to also effectively influence them for Christ. The wheel began to turn. My capacities would increase, which would then drive me back to God, soliciting further growth in character to fit my new responsibilities.

I think most Christian leaders experience this dynamic. There is an initial moment when we realize that serving God is impossible unless he continues to outfit us for the journey. But the real challenge is in holding on to this lesson through all the varied stages of life. As we gain capacity, we become targets for unique pressures, temptations, and distractions that threaten to burn us out, shift our focus, or quietly undermine the substance of our character. We must learn not just how to grow but also how to guard our capacity for impact and sustain a lifetime of joyful service.

15

The Traps That Hinder Growth

Guarding Your Capacity for Impact

A vessel under construction remains a long time on
the stocks, but when launched on the ocean of life, its
speed and stability are soon tested.
J. OSWALD SANDERS

IT'S ROUGH OUT here for those of us who still skateboard past the
age of thirty-seven.

First off, the injury and recovery cycle doesn't move as fast as it
used to. One bad landing typically means a few weeks off my board
these days.

Second, my prefrontal cortex is now fully developed.
Advancing in skateboarding requires a total suspension of reason

and relatively low inhibitions. Seriously, what clear-minded person would fasten a pair of wheels to a wooden slat, prop it up against the edge of a fifteen-foot-deep concrete bowl, and intentionally fall forward at a near 90-degree angle?

It also certainly helps if you're nineteen, have no kids to provide for, and are smugly certain you'll live forever.

I do love the sport, but truth be told, my ability lags behind my enthusiasm; my skill level is barely intermediate. Sadly, I can't fully blame my age. Even though I started skating at eleven, I refused to learn some of the basic mechanics needed for more advanced tricks until I was in my late twenties. I also didn't ride for almost eight years during what was probably my physical peak.

And so, when you add it all up, my current limitations aren't that surprising. I'll bet a good instructor could have evaluated me ten years ago and easily predicted where I'd be today if my approach didn't change.

Why Time Alone Won't Produce Mastery

Listen to your coaches: Form and developmental stages matter.

If you are seeking to grow or to master a skill, you can seemingly afford to neglect certain lessons early on. But eventually, these missing pieces of your foundation become painfully apparent. It's easy to assume that the longer you do something, the better you will be. But time and effort on their own don't produce masters.

Christian character growth, and the leadership that arises from it, isn't exactly like skateboarding, or really any other skill for that matter. But it is dynamic and happens in stages. This growth is not always linear; plateaus and setbacks are a normal part of the process. And just because you worked hard at it a long time ago doesn't mean you will continue to improve.

Everyone changes over time, but not always for the better. In the Christian life, even for those in leadership, it's possible to forfeit hard-fought and long-held ground, jeopardizing not just our own character but also the health of our ministry.

What gets in the way of continued progress for a leader? In this chapter, we consider common stumbling blocks and how to avoid them, including the struggle with *spiritual pride*, the trap of *legalism*, the danger of *lopsided growth*, the slow decay of *mission drift*, and the necessity of forming proper *responses to suffering*.

Spiritual Pride

Self-righteousness can slip in the back door after success of any kind, and ministry is no exception. As our professional or spiritual competencies increase, we get used to feeling in control. It's easy to assume we are entitled to continued success, and that's when complacency can set in.

Spiritually mature people know that regression and stagnation are dangers at any stage. We never "arrive." In fact, people who see themselves as having arrived demonstrate remarkable immaturity. Remaining teachable means we have to keep learning humility right up until our dying day.

Spiritual pride reveals itself in specific ways:

- Refusing to learn from others, especially those with less experience or fewer credentials.
- Reacting poorly to new challenges or just avoiding them altogether.
- Becoming proud and self-assured to the point of neglecting peers and partners.
- Developing a critical spirit toward anyone who does things differently.

J. Oswald Sanders warns that there is a spiritual equivalent to aging and senility that has nothing to do with our physical age:

> It is a solemnizing fact that we can "unknow" truth which we have once apprehended, and which once gripped and enthralled us. Any Christian who has seriously backslidden is very conscious of this. The writer of the letter to the Hebrews emphasizes this possibility. "You have become dull of hearing. When for the time you ought to be teachers, you have become such as need someone to teach you" (Heb. 5:11–12). They were not always dull of hearing, the correct tense of the verb suggests. Once they were responsive to the truth, but now they have degenerated into spiritual senility.[1]

This is the subtle tragedy of spiritual pride: It convinces us to stop the hard work of growth because we think we've already finished. This was the attitude of the Laodicean Christians, whom Jesus directly addresses in Revelation 3:17: "You say, 'I am rich; I have acquired wealth and do not need a thing.' But you do not realize that you are wretched, pitiful, poor, blind and naked."

Spiritual pride is defeated by cultivating humility in every stage of life and ministry. Even if we've learned a thing or two and accomplished certain spiritual goals, how much credit can we really take in good conscience? We all stand on the shoulders of those who came before us. We owe any fruit or wisdom in our lives to the Giver of all good things. Humble people see clearly how even their best works are like "filthy rags" (Isaiah 64:6), and, if anything, are amazed at the ways that God has chosen to use them.

Properly understood, humility is strength. It causes us to depend more deeply on Christ. Spiritual pride, on the other hand, is evil and one of Satan's best tools for making sure that early leadership impact never matures into a deep, long-lasting, and Spirit-filled ministry.

Legalism

Legalism often overflows from spiritual pride. When we believe our efforts have made us superior or "finished," the logical next step is to build a system of rules—legalism—to maintain that perceived superiority.

Willful, carnal sin is damaging, but legalism kills character growth in its own special way. It's an obsession with rules and outward appearances that actively prevents inward spiritual transformation. God's renovating work goes to the very bones, while legalism is content with cosmetics.

Legalism is similar to a sick person treating symptoms while avoiding all the root causes of their disease. Someone with a bad case of pneumonia doesn't just need an over-the-counter cough suppressant. She needs heavy steroids to clear out the inflammation in her lungs.

Over time, a works-centered approach to spirituality leads to fakery and burnout. Joy is sapped when our sense of right standing with God fluctuates according to our performance.

Legalism can show up in a variety of ways:

- Deriving a sense of righteousness from our ministry efforts, spiritual rhythms, or practices.
- Prioritizing external obedience in others over genuine heart-level transformation.
- Excusing our own attitudinal sins (like bitterness or careerism) while emphasizing and judging the more outward failings of others.

One of the Bible's most vivid examples of legalism is found in the older brother in the Parable of the Prodigal Son (Luke 15). When the younger son returns, the older brother—who never physically left home—is furious. He confronts his father with a works-based scorecard: "Look! All these years I've been slaving for you and never disobeyed your orders. Yet you never gave me even a young goat so I could celebrate with my friends" (v.29). The older brother viewed his obedience as transactional (serving as a hired hand, not a son) and viewed grace as unfair. His legalism made him miserable and isolated, tragically unwilling to join the celebration.

The New Testament reserves some of its sharpest rebukes for issues of legalism. If you read Galatians and Hebrews all the way through, you'll see that both groups were caught in the trap of ritualism and had returned to a rigid, rules-based approach to relating to God. They had forgotten that everything God provides is a gift of grace and is received through faith. Interestingly, those early Christians, for the most part, weren't compromising with the world's values when it came to money or sex. Instead, religious legalism was at the root of their backsliding.

Real character change requires the freedom that comes from consciously operating under God's gift of grace. We overcome legalism by embracing our status as accepted, beloved children of God. Only when we're in touch with God's unconditional love can we look in the mirror and have the courage to face what we see.

Spiritual life begins and continues through the power of God alone. Paul pleads, "I would like to learn just one thing from you: Did you receive the Spirit by the works of the law, or by believing what you heard? Are you so foolish? After beginning by means of the Spirit, are you now trying to finish by means of the flesh?" (Galatians 3:2–3).

Lopsided Growth

Uneven development happens when we allow God to work on certain parts of our hearts while boxing him out of others. We become like aspiring powerlifters who only work out one arm and skip "leg day"! Sometimes, such uneven growth does not become apparent until years down the line, but its impact on leadership is profound, eroding both personal integrity and team trust.

Things like secret bitterness, nursed lust, or subtle materialism can remain hidden in damp corners of our hearts and hinder us from further spiritual growth, creating blind spots that inevitably lead to inconsistent, confusing, or even harmful leadership decisions. An example of this is found in the imagery of Revelation 3:20: "Here I am! I stand at the door and knock. If anyone hears my voice and opens the door, I will come in and eat with that person, and they with me." We often employ this vivid illustration to explain receiving Jesus into your heart. But the original context for this verse is Jesus' address to the seven established churches of Asia Minor. With all but two churches, Jesus affirms their many admirable qualities. But then he goes on to say, "But I have this against you." These churches were guilty of major oversights. They had let the Holy Spirit lead them in the past, but to survive and flourish, they would need to go further and address these shortcomings or face the natural consequences.

Graciously, God often chooses to work around the things we aren't ready to hand over. But we can't put off letting Jesus in forever. He is more than a guest who eats, chats about music and the weather, and then leaves at a reasonable hour. When we invite Jesus into our lives, he moves in. Naturally, he wants access to every part of the house. Our refusal to grant him that full access results in us carrying dead weight. Hebrews 12:1–2 urges us, "Therefore, since we are surrounded by such a great cloud of witnesses, let us throw off everything that hinders and the sin that so easily entangles. And let us run with perseverance the race marked out for us, fixing our eyes on Jesus, the pioneer and perfecter of faith."

Imagine trying to run in a race while carrying a microwave. You could stubbornly argue, "Hey, I am still making progress! It's not like I'm not running!" Sure, buddy. But you would gain considerable stamina and speed if you left that dead weight behind. You'd also look less silly! The same is true of our sin: We may make some progress while holding on to certain areas, but we will make much more progress if we surrender them to God.

Lopsided growth can result from a transactional attitude toward our spirituality. We argue, "I have given God X, Y, and Z … therefore I'm justified in holding T, U, V, and W!" But this attitude is nothing short of plain old religious legalism. We deserve nothing from God and are in no position to make demands.

Rather than holding back, we should surrender our whole lives to God. It's the only thing that makes sense, considering who God is and the nature of our relationship to him: "Nothing in all creation is hidden from God's sight. Everything is uncovered and laid bare before the eyes of him to whom we must give account" (Hebrews 4:13). For a leader, this truth demands a higher level of accountability, as our unaddressed flaws will affect not only ourselves but also those we lead.

The good news is that we don't face this scrutiny alone. The author of Hebrews immediately follows this warning by offering the antidote to shame and fear:

> Therefore, since we have a great high priest who has ascended into heaven, Jesus the Son of God, let us hold firmly to the faith we profess. For we do not have a high priest who is unable to empathize with our weaknesses, but we have one who has been tempted in every way, just as we are—yet he did not sin. Let us then approach God's throne of grace with confidence, so that we may receive mercy and find grace to help us in our time of need.
>
> HEBREWS 4:14–16

This grace gives us the courage to honestly look at the "raw side" of our character. We must be willing to let God expose what is hidden.

If we observe ourselves doing any of the following, we may be experiencing lopsided growth:

- Seeing an underdeveloped aspect of our character (such as self-discipline, discernment, intercessory prayer) become a critical roadblock to health and progress in our ministry.
- Acting out or giving into sin when experiencing abnormal pressures and difficulties.
- Experiencing burnout, which can suggest we haven't grown in our ability to draw on the Lord for power, guidance, and spiritual replenishment.[2]

Illustrating the danger of lopsided spiritual growth, J. Oswald Sanders turns to the prophet Hosea, who uses a vivid, unforgettable image from the kitchen. It's so good that I can't help but quote it at length.

> "Ephraim is a cake not turned" (7:8). This was a pictorial figure familiar to Israel. What [baker] has not had the humiliating experience of a cake cooked on the outside but half-raw within? The cake referred to here was cooked on a griddle, and not having been turned, it was burned on one side and raw on the other. Many are like this in character—overdeveloped in some respects but deficient in others. Progress has been excellent in some areas but retarded in others. All of us to some extent are only partially sanctified, because we have not turned some parts of our lives toward the fire of the Holy Spirit. Some are strong in Bible knowledge but weak in spiritual grace. Some are generous in nature but violent in temper. Some are strong for orthodoxy but weak in Christian love. One-sided development is true of us

all. Jesus alone was completely sanctified and truly symmetrical in character, "full of grace and truth." In Him we see in perfect balance "the goodness and severity of God." It could never be said of Him that He was "a cake not turned."

It is a common temptation to overdo some form of work which we like, but to neglect hidden and less congenial tasks. We tend to cultivate our strong points and to neglect our weak ones. The scholar avidly feeds his mind but neglects his body. Scripture enjoins the cultivation of the weak points in our characters, so that we may "stand perfect and complete in all the will of God."

The reassuring fact for us is that the fire under the cake still burns. There is yet time for the cake to be turned and for the baking process to be completed. It is for us to turn the imperfect, unfinished part of our characters toward the fire of the Spirit and allow Him to sanctify us wholly.[3]

It's encouraging to know it's never too late to grow—the fire under the cake still burns. Lopsided growth is the result of selective surrender, so to counter it, we have to choose total surrender. If God makes you aware of an area of weakness, don't be embarrassed. Surrender it to him, and praise him that even in this later stage he is dedicated to seeing you become all he made you to be.

We also must understand that lopsided growth is inevitable because spiritual growth never happens evenly or all at once. God is so gracious to us and works around our missteps and immaturity. If he didn't work this way, then none of us would be able to serve him while we are young and inexperienced. But he regularly chooses the weak and foolish things of the world to shame the wise! He doesn't call leaders ready-made; he makes us along the way. The key is remaining humble in the midst of our inadequacy and responding earnestly when we sense the Spirit drawing us to a new area of change.

Mission Drift

If a ship isn't properly moored, the tide will gradually pull it down the coast or out to sea. In a similar way, Christian workers tragically lose direction and drift away from the center of their calling. This sort of drift is disconcerting because it doesn't happen suddenly. It happens slowly as a person's core convictions weaken, and as a result, their mission subtly shifts. The same can be said for organizations. Peter Greer and Chris Horst address this issue in their influential book *Mission Drift*:

> Without careful attention, faith-based organizations will inevitably drift from their founding mission. It's that simple. It will happen. Slowly, silently, and with little fanfare, organizations routinely drift from their original purpose, and most will never return to their original intent. It has happened repeatedly throughout history.[4]

Greer and Horst name several culprits for mission drift, including but not limited to caving to cultural pressure, neglecting prayer, being spoiled by success, and inattention to kingdom results. Legitimate but secondary goals are gradually elevated and eventually eclipse gospel faithfulness. Serving the poor and building communities takes precedence over sharing the message of Jesus, when in fact the two should be indispensably intertwined (Luke 4:18–19, 9:2).

Countess biblical stories reveal how even once-vital spiritual leaders can lose their way. King Asa is a prime example of mission drift at work (2 Chronicles 16). Asa took the throne as a young man and immediately led the nation in spiritual reform, even deposing his own idol-worshipping grandmother! But down the road, he faltered. Faced with an enemy, he drifted from his faith and his mission by taking silver and gold from the temple and paid off a foreign king of Aram to help, rather than relying on God. His plan initially worked. But God knew this move represented a change in Asa's heart, so he sent the prophet Hanani to say:

> Because you relied on the king of Aram and not on the Lord your God, the army of the king of Aram has escaped from your hand. Were not the Cushites and Libyans a mighty army with great numbers of chariots and horsemen? Yet when you relied on the Lord, he delivered them into your hand. For the eyes of the Lord range throughout the earth to strengthen those whose hearts are fully committed to him. You have done a foolish thing, and from now on you will be at war.
>
> 2 CHRONICLES 16:7–9

Asa responded poorly to God's rebuke. He oppressed his people during his final years and threw Hanani in prison! What happened? Asa had been spoiled by success and neglected the spiritual lessons of his youth. He forgot that his mission as God's appointed king wasn't just to protect Judah and cause it to prosper materially but also to protect and prosper the kingdom spiritually, through modeling reliance on the Lord. Asa's story is a prime example of mission drift at work: a strategic lure diverting him from his original, most essential purpose. Pastor and teacher Dennis McCallum points out,

> Satan deceives leaders, not just for personal pleasure but mainly in order to divert them from their mission. Christian history is littered with examples of the church devoting itself to projects that have nothing to do with our central mission and that actually discredit it. Diversion is his plan for you also. He may not be able to talk you into doing something crazy (like burning people at the stake or publicly whipping sinners), but if he directs your efforts toward ineffective pursuits, he wins.[5]

Satan's strategy of diversion helps explain the tragic late-career stumbles of many public Christian leaders. When recent scandals involving sex and money erupt, we watch in horror and ask, *What happened?* The answer is rarely simple, but the pastor caught in an affair wasn't struck by lightning, which then made them sin. There is always a slow, private process of temptation and compromise that leads to the moment of failure. Before we make large compromises, we usually make small ones. Letting go of core values and beneficial practices happens gradually, but a post-mortem spiritual analysis typically reveals the warning signs were there for quite some time. King David's sordid affair with Bathsheba didn't begin that day on the rooftop. It began when he abandoned his primary mission as king by deciding to retire his sword and let others fight in his place.

This slow decay of focus leads to mission drift—we're likely experiencing this if we find ourselves doing any of the following:

- Investing more in building a platform (rubbing shoulders with elites, networking, consulting, attending specialized conferences) than doing less glamorous, ground-level kingdom work (investing in core community, disciple-making, serving the poor).
- Letting go of personal time in prayer and Scripture in favor of self-help books or social- media-driven Christian fads.
- Speaking more and more of our past service and accomplishments, rather than being lit up by the fresh things God is doing in and through us.

The Great Commission orients all Christian service: "Therefore go and make disciples of all nations, baptizing them in the name of the Father and of the Son and of the Holy Spirit, and teaching them to obey everything I have commanded you" (Matthew 28:19–20). Jesus' marching orders to his disciples are our north star too. It's the marker by which we should assess all our ministry activity. Are disciples truly being made? Are we winning the lost to faith in Christ? Are we teaching all that Christ commanded? If we take Jesus seriously, then these questions must remain central in all we do.

Organizations sometimes pay for external audits to maintain high standards of transparency. Spiritually, we should similarly welcome being audited on occasion—even when the process feels inconvenient and painful. At times, God will also send in prophetic voices to challenge and reorient us back to our calling, just like he did for ancient Israel. This is one reason it's important to engage with believers outside our immediate networks. We are all prone to building feedback loops that affirm and reaffirm our decisions. But people who aren't as involved in our systems can more clearly see our shortcomings.

If you lead a church or organization, make sure you cultivate this kind of missional accountability with other ministry leaders in your area. We are more likely to stay on course if we run together.

Poor Responses to Suffering

Jesus promised power and companionship to his disciples, but he never offered total deliverance from the effects of a sinful world. He said, "I have told you these things, so that in me you may have peace. In this world you will have trouble. But take heart! I have overcome the world" (John 16:33).

Far from being immune to the pain this world inflicts, believers are sometimes *more* exposed to it as they devote themselves to ministry. This side of heaven contains inescapable tragedy. Loved ones die. Goals go unreached. Hopes are frustrated. Such moments have the power to shatter faith or at least dull our excitement for service. We need solid theology and patterns for spiritual living that enable us to weather inevitable suffering.

Developing a solid theology of suffering begins with establishing biblical expectations. We shouldn't be blindsided by hardship. Peter told his friends, "Do not be surprised at the fiery ordeal that has come on you to test you, as though something strange were happening to you" (1 Peter 4:12).

James, the brother of Jesus and early Christian martyr, advised, "Consider it pure joy, my brothers and sisters, whenever you face trials of many kinds, because you know that the testing of your faith produces perseverance. Let perseverance finish its work so that you may be mature and complete, not lacking anything" (James 1:2–4). Trials met with faith form us more than any program ever could.

A healthy approach to suffering means believing that, despite the odds, God's power will overcome! Our goal isn't just to *survive* painful circumstances. Rather, we should spiritually flourish because of them. As Paul says,

> Therefore we do not lose heart. Though outwardly we are wasting away, yet inwardly we are being renewed day by day. For our light and momentary troubles are achieving for us an eternal glory that far outweighs them all. So we fix our eyes not on what is seen, but on what is unseen, since what is seen is temporary, but what is unseen is eternal.
>
> 2 CORINTHIANS 4:16–18

Christians are sometimes dumbfounded when God seemingly says no to earnest prayers for reprieve. Although his reasons for allowing pain can be mysterious, God never neglects to work in the life of the person who encounters suffering and chooses to trust in him. Even Paul begged God to take away an evil that seemed to hinder his life and ministry. Mysteriously, God decided to leave the problem right where it was, but he did give Paul something else, saying, "My grace is sufficient for you, for my power is made perfect in weakness" (2 Corinthians 12:9).

These frustrating limitations led Paul into deep lessons about day-to-day reliance on the power and grace of God. He goes on to say, "I will boast all the more gladly about my weaknesses, so that Christ's power may rest on me. That is why, for Christ's sake, I delight in weaknesses, in insults, in hardships, in persecutions, in difficulties. For when I am weak, then I am strong" (2 Corinthians 12:9–10). The Lord knew Paul needed the spiritual insight that came through suffering more than he needed rescue from the suffering itself.

That's a hard truth to swallow when it comes our way.

When my daughter was young, she suffered extreme night terrors. She would scream and run around during the night, sometimes hurting herself. These episodes robbed my wife and me of sleep and energy, and we repeatedly asked God to stop them. I don't know why God allowed these to continue. But I do know that on the nights they happened, I would lay awake in prayer. I was also driven to be vulnerable and emotional with the people I was leading at the time. Like Paul, my own weakness became the surprising source of greater reliance on God and stronger connection to others.

Suffering needs to be interpreted spiritually. Unfortunately, our most reflexive responses to pain are spiritually destructive rather than spiritually fruitful. One misguided reflex to pain is to move toward the error of asceticism. The ascetic believes that all pain is good and productive. Pleasure, according to them, is generally unhealthy or unspiritual. This kind of thinking quickly emerged among early Christians only a century after Jesus. Even Christian leaders like Origen believed self-mutilation was an expression of piety.[6] He went the full distance and castrated himself to demonstrate devotion and prevent lust.

Before you run for the hills, understand this philosophy is unbiblical and perverse. While the writers of Scripture acknowledge the role suffering can play in spiritual growth, they never glorify suffering for its own sake. Paul said, "I have learned the secret of being content in any and every situation, whether well fed or hungry, whether living in plenty or in want. I can do all this through him who gives me strength" (Philippians 4:12–13). Notice Paul doesn't disparage the good times. His point is that in Christ he has the capacity to live fulfilled no matter the circumstances.

How we react to hardship says a lot. Most of us can be generous and kind with a clear horizon and wind in our sails. It's the times of uncertainty that showcase what's going on inside. J. Oswald Sanders comments:

> The spiritually immature person meets adult situations and tests with childish and immature reactions…. This always produces tension and strain with all the attendant problems. When sorrow strikes, he is inclined to indulge in an orgy of self-centered emotion. If financial reverses occur, he is at a loss to know why this should come to him, and he blames God. When hopes are dashed, he loses heart and drops his bundle. When adversity overtakes him, he is swallowed up in self-pity. In domestic difficulties he indulges in tantrums or sulks and creates an atmosphere that mars home unity. When placed with other difficult people, he falls prey to censorious criticism and "gives as good as he gets." When his will is thwarted by God or man, he becomes rebellious and bitter. So then our spiritual maturity or immaturity is seen in the manner in which we react to the changing circumstances of life.[7]

Suffering tests the depth of a leader's character. We may be on the run from what God wants to teach us if we find ourselves doing any of the following:

- Avoiding painful situations at all costs, even if it means abandoning key relationships.
- Dealing with stress by falling back on short-term relief strategies like excessive eating, screen addiction, video games, or alcohol.
- Blaming God and others for our circumstances, spending inordinate amounts of time stuck in self-pity, and growing bitter.

Sanders says those who embrace adverse circumstances stand to gain much: "God will use the friction of adverse circumstances rightly received to impart a sharp cutting edge to His servant's ministry."[8]

But if the goal of the Christian life is to become Christlike, then we have stumbled across an amazing truth. The Christian life is undefeatable! God's plan for us is certain as long as we remain under the protection of his wings. Corrie ten Boom said, "Every experience God gives us ... is the perfect preparation for a future only He can see."[9]

However, it is crucial not to mistake this spiritual certainty for emotional denial. The Christian life is undefeatable because of Christ's power, not because we are somehow immune to pain or grief. To be mature is to bring our true, whole selves—including our wounds, confusion, and despair—before God. Only when we honestly acknowledge the pain can we engage in the spiritual work that leads to growth and enables us to impact others. Yale Theologian Miroslav Volf says,

> Rage belongs before God—not in the reflectively managed and manicured form of a confession, but as a prereflective outburst from the depths of the soul.... [B]y placing unattended rage before God we place both our unjust enemy and our own vengeful self face-to-face with a God who loves and does justice.[10]

As Volf counsels, our response to suffering should include laying all our feelings before God. Prayer is the safest and most productive place that exists to pour out the unfiltered contents of our hearts.

Constructive suffering happens best in community. We make a tragic mistake when we allow suffering to isolate us from others. Satan's checkmate is to get us alone. Being alone in a dark room surrounded by screens isn't a path forward. It's a prison! It's during times of deep suffering that we most need our spouses, families, and friends. We should also take advantage of professional, biblically informed counseling when it is available. This is why the preacher of Ecclesiastes reasons,

> Two are better than one, because they have a good return for their labor: If either of them falls down, one can help the other up. But pity anyone who falls and has no one to help them up. Also, if two lie down together, they will keep warm. But how can one keep warm alone? Though one may be overpowered, two can defend themselves. A cord of three strands is not quickly broken.
>
> ECCLESIASTES 4:9–12

When hard times hit, the temptation to grow bitter and resentful is powerful. We feel like our lives are on pause until we can escape the person, place, or circumstance causing irritation and pain. But we must be careful in these moments. Trying to rush our way out of problems may be circumventing God's plan. Similar to the way diamonds are formed, certain levels of spiritual formation require extreme pressure.

Character growth isn't ensuring we never encounter these stumbling blocks. Committed disciples of Jesus will likely face every last one. Navigating seasons of spiritual regression with humility is part of walking faithfully with God.

Repeatedly, the authors of Scripture compare the Christian life to a race. Charting your obstacles is an important part of running a race, but it isn't the race itself. Ultimately, it's God's power and abundant grace that pulls us over the finish line. Our goal is to stay on the path and run our race well, trusting God to do the rest. From this position, we can then effectively guide and encourage those running alongside us.

The Sustaining Disciplines

Habits for the Long Haul

It is only by this fidelity in small matters that the grace
of true love is sustained and distinguished from the
transitory excitements of nature.

FRANÇOIS FÉNELON

IT'S INCREDIBLE HOW certain athletes are able to keep playing
elite-level sport well past their prime. Think of Lebron James who,
in his forties, still puts up dominant NBA performances. Even more
impressive are people like Mathea Allansmith, who completed a
marathon at the age of ninety-two.[1] Interviews with athletes who
continue to compete despite the wear and tear of aging reveal that their
success can be attributed to more than just stellar genetics. They are

128

disciplined people, who understand how to pace themselves, conserve energy, and live in such a way that makes their exertion sustainable. Their routines ensure that their minds stay sharp and their bodies limber.

A Long Obedience in the Same Direction

Pressing on in developing Christlike character is not so different. If we want to persevere, fulfill our calling, and make it to the end, we need a mindset like Paul's. We have seen throughout this book how he consistently compares the Christian life to a long-distance race (Philippians 3:12–14, 1 Corinthians 9:24–27, 2 Timothy 4:7).

At the end of a marathon, the human body is spent. Even the pros collapse at the finish line. The same will be true for our lives here on earth. We will all ultimately run out of energy, and be gathered to our Lord. But it's up to us to meter our lives and adopt spiritual disciplines to keep us going for the long haul. These disciplines aren't in and of themselves aspects of character; rather, they are helpful habits that keep us fit and running on the right path, ensuring we finish well.

A helpful way to learn about such spiritual disciplines is to consider the examples of leaders who have gone before us. God tells us to pay careful attention to the lives of spiritually mature men and women. Hebrews 13:7 tells us, "Remember your leaders, who spoke the word of God to you. Consider the outcome of their way of life and imitate their faith."

This chapter looks at key disciplines that have been practiced in the lives of effectual ordinary leaders throughout the ages— *regular study, daily fellowship with God, committed friendship, simple living,* and *gratitude.*

We can read about many Christian leaders who embodied these disciplines in numerous inspiring biographies, but let's not neglect the living letters (2 Corinthians 3:2–3) right in front of us. Proverbs exhorts us to "Walk with the wise and become wise" (Proverbs 13:20). Not everyone has the privilege of learning from wise people in their local context, but those who do should take full advantage.

Regular Study

Mature leaders are learners. I've never met a seasoned spiritual leader who seemed satisfied with their existing knowledge; they absorb new material with hunger and seek out fresh ways to be spiritually sharpened. Total enlightenment isn't a Christian objective. As I argued earlier, we never fully arrive. Heaven itself will be spent plumbing the eternal depths of God's being (Romans 11:33). Rather than growing satiated with life, mature people seem to increasingly realize they have only just begun to live.

Part of the reason learning must never cease is because ministry contexts are always changing. While human nature is constant, human culture is always in flux. It's important to keep pace with the times. When we lose touch with what people around us think, we become less able to communicate Christ in comprehendible ways. As theologian and pastor Francis Schaeffer observed, "It is our task to speak to our generation; the past has gone, the future is not yet here. So the positive side of apologetics is the communication of the Gospel to the present generation in terms that they can understand."[2]

Today, gospel communication is especially challenging due to political tribalism and misinformation through consumer media sources. There is a desperate need for Christians to be differentiated by an evident commitment to truth outside themselves.

This is one reason it's so important to keep learning in the context of *community*. Reading in isolation has its uses, but if practiced exclusively, it can result in faulty premises and untested conclusions.

Leaders who grow in influence often tend to lose proximity with their spiritual peers. We shouldn't leave this work to annual conferences or yearly retreats. Establishing a regular time and place to connect, read, and discuss challenging material helps keep leaders sharp. Build rigorous study with others into your life. Although it's good to fellowship, share personally, and tell stories with friends, be careful not to lose the sharp edge that comes from learning together as well.

Ultimately, reading all the books in the world and listening to every podcast won't matter if we neglect God's Word. Spending time each day absorbing God's thoughts through Scripture is a basic reflex to abiding. So often when a leader shipwrecks, they confess in tears that time spent studying God's Word disappeared months or even years before.

Questions for Reflection

- What am I currently learning, and alongside whom?
- What are my best sources for being personally sharpened?
- How do I challenge myself with new ideas?

Daily Fellowship with God

Learning new information is important. Studying God's Word matters even more. However, academic exercise doesn't guarantee a living connection with God. We must study Scripture, but we need to go even further: We must open our hearts in faith in order to receive truth and blessing through the Holy Spirit.

Mature Christians practice meditative prayer. Intercessory prayer for others and supplication for personal needs can be woven in, but the key is quieting your thoughts and reflectively taking your seat before God. This practice invites him to both lead and fill you with his presence.

In presenting ourselves as empty, we can receive spiritual comfort and power. Watchman Nee states,

> What is the secret strength of the Christian life? Whence has it its power? Let me give you the answer in a sentence: The Christian's secret is in his rest in Christ. His power derives from his God-given position. All who sit can walk, for in the thought of God the one follows the other spontaneously. We sit forever with Christ that we may walk continuously before men. Forsake for a moment our place of rest in him, and immediately we are tripped and our testimony in the world is marred. But abide in Christ, and our position there ensures the power to walk worthy of him here.[3]

All of Christian experience flows from where we stand with Jesus. But the wear and tear of each day so easily separates us from what we know to be true. Daily reorientation is therefore necessary—like a navigator using the stars each night to confirm her ship's position.

Most of us find it easier and beneficial to meet with God in the mornings before engaging with the stress the day brings. The most important thing is to spend with God whatever time you have, free from distractions.

Easier said than done! We are all immersed in a consumer culture deliberately structured to steal our attention and reshape our life patterns. If we don't deliberately carve out regular time and establish disciplines that make knowing God our first priority, we will absolutely be swept away. Pastor and cultural analyst Mark Sayers warns,

Vast amounts of time and money are spent by corporations and tech giants to arrange our life architecture to suit their goals. The life system of the average person in the West is now primarily shaped around the patterns set by our phones to harvest information to be sold for profit, as well as influencing us to purchase particular goods and experiences. Our life patterns have become one of the great battlegrounds of the contemporary world.[4]

For any of us who are unsure how to find quiet and focus on their new identity in Christ, Andrew Murray's template for "Daily Fellowship with God" is an excellent primer. Check it out in appendix two at the end of this book.

Questions for Reflection

- Where do I go to be truly alone with God?
- What steps am I taking to preserve this time and cut away distractions?
- How can I start each day assured of who I am in Christ?

Committed Friendship

Fellowship with other Christians is a blessing, not a right. Dietrich Bonhoeffer was correct when he highlighted the rarity and privilege of community:

It is not simply to be taken for granted that the Christian has the privilege of living among other Christians. Jesus Christ lived in the midst of his enemies. At the end all his disciples deserted him. On the Cross he was utterly alone, surrounded by evildoers and mockers. For this cause he had come, to bring peace to the enemies of God…. So between the death of Christ and the Last Day it is only by a gracious anticipation of the last things that Christians are privileged to live in visible fellowship with other Christians. It is by the grace of God that a congregation is permitted to gather visibly in this world to share God's Word and sacrament. Not all Christians receive this blessing.[5]

Thankfully, the Holy Spirit is truly sufficient for those isolated in prison, sickness, or mission. If any of us were left with none but Jesus, he would still be capable of meeting our deepest needs.

That being said, the biblical wisdom of keeping close friendships is loud and clear. "How good and pleasant it is when God's people live together in unity" (Psalm 133:1). "A friend loves at all times and a brother is born for adversity" (Proverbs 17:17). We need consistent and committed peer relationships to equip, encourage, and hold us accountable through each season of life. "As iron sharpens iron so one person sharpens another" (Proverbs 27:17).

Too often, as responsibilities multiply, friendship diminishes. Christian workers can become so preoccupied with their families and personal ministry that they neglect key relationships. The wisest men and women I know have close relationships that span decades. Ajith Fernando argues that leaders need good friends and peers for emotional health and security:

Just to be able to relax in the company of people we can trust helps reduce the pain of ministry. Sharing our problems and disappointments with sympathetic friends helps combat the tendency for us to be bitter and angry people. … It distresses me how so many leaders say that they can't take the risk of nurturing close friendships because they fear it will result in hurt and betrayal. Early in his Christian walk John Wesley went to see someone he described as "a serious man" who told him: "Sir, you wish to serve God and go to heaven? Remember you cannot serve him alone. You must therefore find companions

> or make them; the Bible knows nothing of solitary religion."
> … Friends help us avoid many of the dangers associated with
> discipling ministry.[6]

We must surround ourselves with people who know our strengths and are realistic about our faults. Leaders are often tempted to seek out the company of those most impressed by their charisma and achievements. Remember the wisdom of Proverbs: "Wounds from a friend can be trusted, but an enemy multiplies kisses" (Proverbs 27:6). Consider periodically reaffirming to your friends that they have an open invitation to examine your life and speak their minds. Keep choosing the people who challenge you.

Questions for Reflection

- Who are my accountability partners?
- Who knows me best and is able to speak into my life when necessary?
- What can I do to strengthen these relationships?

Simple Living

Simple living is the biblical alternative to materialism. It involves choosing a decluttered life centered on God and people rather than on money, experiences, worldly achievements, and things.

Simple living is more than an attitude; it's a strategic rebellion against the world system ruled by Satan. It requires cultivating biblical convictions about what matters most and investing our time and energy into spiritual things. Wars aren't won by good intentions. No one succeeds at simple living without making concrete lifestyle changes and setting specific goals in areas like giving, budgeting, and the wise use of our existing financial and material resources.

For spiritual leaders, simple living must be more than a matter of private discipline—it must be visible to others. Otherwise, our values won't be imitable. This plays out in morally gray decisions like how much money to spend on a house or the type of clothes we wear. While we must avoid rigid rules or contrived standards, mature leaders are mindful of what their purchases and possessions communicate.

We live in a world where people are quick to write off faith leaders as money-hungry hypocrites. It's hard to blame them for doing so! Simple living offers a chance to earn credibility. A mentor of mine was once accused online of being a greedy megachurch pastor. Reluctantly, some of the man's own critics came to his defense! The slander simply didn't stick. He drove a junky car and lived in a modest home. This is what it means for a leader to be "above reproach" (1 Timothy 3:2).

Simple living is a deliberate choice and is fundamentally different from being miserly. Stingy people are just as selfish as exorbitant spenders. The difference lies in their motivations. Misers usually seek security, while spenders are driven by stimulation. Neither type of person looks to God to meet their needs. Instead, true generosity grows through trusting in his provision.

> Now he who supplies seed to the sower and bread for food will also supply and increase your store of seed and will enlarge the harvest of your righteousness. You will be enriched in every way so that you can be generous on every occasion, and through us your generosity will result in thanksgiving to God.
>
> 2 CORINTHIANS 9:10–11

This biblical promise defines our responsibility: The ultimate point of being "enriched in every way" is to use worldly wealth for God's purposes. Of course, these purposes include providing for our families and even enjoying some entertainment and rest. But we should view everything we have as assets to be invested, with the ultimate payoff coming in eternity. Commenting on Jesus' Parable of the Shrewd Manager in Luke 16:8–10, Randy Alcorn asks,

> Whom have we influenced spiritually to the point that they would welcome us into their eternal dwelling places? To which needy people have we sacrificially given our resources to the glory of God? Every time we give to world missions, famine relief, prison ministry, and Bible translation, whenever we invest our time and prayers, we can dream about the day we'll meet and enjoy the hospitality of new friends and family, precious people in Heaven. One day, money will be useless. While it's still useful, God's money managers with foresight will use it for eternal good.[7]

Later, Alcorn points out, "A life centered on money and possessions is not only misguided; it's utterly self-destructive. It's not only wrong; it's stupid. In stark contrast, the Christ-centered life is not only right; it's smart. It sometimes pays off in the short run, and it always pays off in the long run."[8]

When I asked a seasoned Christian leader what two forces were most damaging to Christians' spiritual lives over time, he named bitterness and materialism. "Both are deadly because of their stealth," he told me. "They grow by increments and subtly displace God in a person's heart."

Money itself isn't evil. But Paul says the love and pursuit of money is ruinous:

> Those who want to get rich fall into temptation and a trap and into many foolish and harmful desires that plunge people into ruin and destruction. For the love of money is a root of all kinds of evil. Some people, eager for money, have wandered from the faith and pierced themselves with many griefs.
>
> 1 TIMOTHY 6:9–10

Questions for Reflection

- Do I err toward being an exorbitant spender or miserly?
- How am I protecting my heart from the love of money?
- How does my current lifestyle and spending demonstrate my priorities to the people I hope to reach?

Gratitude

At first glance, gratitude may not seem like a personal discipline. But anyone who's been at life and leadership for very long can assure you that it absolutely is.

A thankful spirit is particularly critical for a leader because it directly affects their effectiveness and the culture they create. Gratitude shifts a leader's focus from scarcity and complaints to abundance and opportunity. This perspective helps build resilience in their teams, fosters a more positive environment, and provides a powerful witness to the world.

Thankfulness is something that must be cultivated and maintained—otherwise we lose it. This is because life constantly hands us new reasons to be disappointed. Nancy Leigh DeMoss in her book *Choosing Gratitude* says:

> To a significant degree, your emotional, mental, physical, and spiritual well-being, as well as the health and stability of your relationships with others, will be determined by your gratitude quotient. Cultivating a thankful heart is a safeguard against becoming bitter, prickly, and sour. A grateful child of God can't help but be a joyful, peaceful, radiant person.[9]

If this is true, then gratitude must be contended for on an emotional battlefield of challenging relationships and failed projects. Whenever we encounter a setback, God welcomes us to lament and mourn (Psalm 62:8). But like David in the Psalms, we must ultimately return to the praiseworthy realities of God. No matter who has betrayed us or what life throws at us—be it the sting of personal failure, a debilitating illness, or the deepest grief—God is still good and in control (Psalm 55:20–23). Even when walking through the darkest valley, we can thank him for the comfort of his guidance, and the coming certainty of a refreshed soul beside quiet waters (Psalm 23:1–4).

Consistent gratitude to God serves as a vital lens for the leader, enabling us to view our own sinfulness, the flaws of others, and life's broken situations in their proper context. Leaders who neglect this discipline become vulnerable to bitterness. They lose the ability to truly forgive and the emotional freedom needed to move past accumulated hurts. Leaders are especially susceptible to this because they face unique forms of rejection. When things go wrong, angry people often turn on and blame their leaders. Therefore, accepting the risk of rejection must be a recognized cost of leadership. This is part of what it means for us to daily pick up our cross and follow Jesus. But it's only possible to live this way if we are more fixated on the love and faithfulness of God than on the opinions of others.

Earlier I referenced a seasoned leader who named bitterness as one of the two forces that most often destroys Christians' lives. He also argues that ingratitude is a foundational sin that cascades into others over time when left unaddressed:

> An unthankful person feels empty and entitled, which breeds envy, jealousy, self-pity, etc.—and these attitudes breed sinful behaviors and habits that corrupt and enslave us and damage others.... Ingratitude is the mother of sinful attitudes and behaviors, and gratitude is the mother of godly attitudes and behaviors.[10]

Grateful people stand out from the crowd, especially as they get older. Sadly, most individuals descend over time into self-centered caricatures of themselves. In stark contrast, noticeably grateful people become renewing sources of spiritual life to those around them. Their winsome character points others to the sustaining and transforming power of Jesus. As we've established, this is the very essence of fruitful Christian leadership. This is a life that leads.

Questions for Reflection

- When and how do I practice gratitude?
- How will people be able to tell I am a grateful person?
- What can I praise God for today?

Conclusion

Go forward. Go forward in personal attainments,
forward in gifts and grace, forward in fitness for the
work, and forward in conformity to the image of Jesus.
CHARLES HADDON SPURGEON

Years ago, I was working as an extension site coordinator for Trinity Evangelical Divinity School, which was also the seminary where I was studying for my master's degree. One perk of the job was the opportunity to interact with Christian thinkers and speakers who came to teach there.

On one occasion I received an invitation to dinner with Dr. Robert Coleman, author of the influential book *Master Plan of Evangelism*. A few of us met him at a local diner and spent the first part of the evening asking him about his writing and speaking engagements. He gave friendly, candid answers, but after a while, he abruptly ended our questions, crying, "Enough!" Then, he leaned across the table, almost shouting, and directly challenged me: "Tell me about the young men *you* disciple!"

I was taken aback but started to eagerly describe them one by one. Dr. Coleman brimmed with excitement as I described a friend who had recently come to know Christ and our plans to read the

Bible together. When I finished, he said, "Excellent! Now let me tell you about the men I'm working with." He was practically glowing as he described the small band of men he met with weekly for study and prayer. He shared that his hope for them was that they would soon repeat the process by beginning to inspire and teach others as well.

It absolutely rocked me to see a man in his eighties still so sharp and deeply committed to discipling others. I left that dinner buzzing, ready to throw myself back into the work of presenting others complete in Christ.

Die Climbing

When we live a life that leads, it means we commit to the long haul, setting a sustainable yet zealous pace that maximizes our lives for Jesus, because serving God is a continuous calling from which we never retire. Shouldn't we all hope to be a better spiritual teacher, friend, and disciple-maker ten, twenty, or thirty years from now?

I am so grateful for the first generation of Christians in the church where I was first discipled and later began my pastoral ministry. They are living proof that Robert Coleman isn't a spiritual anomaly. It's possible to fight all the way to the finish, just like the apostle Paul:

> For I am already being poured out like a drink offering, and the time for my departure is near. I have fought the good fight, I have finished the race, I have kept the faith. Now there is in store for me the crown of righteousness, which the Lord, the righteous Judge, will award to me on that day—and not only to me, but also to all who have longed for his appearing.
>
> 2 TIMOTHY 4:6–8

We must continuously cultivate the impulse toward growth and improvement—it's essential if we are to spiritually survive.

People of character remain concerned with effectiveness; they want whatever time they have left to count. According to Paul, this attitude isn't human-centered but spiritual and wise: "Be very careful, then, how you live—not as unwise but as wise, making the most of every opportunity, because the days are evil" (Ephesians 5:15–16). Peter agrees: "Prepare your minds for action, keep sober *in spirit*, set your hope completely on the grace to be brought to you at the revelation of Jesus Christ" (1 Peter 1:13 NASB, emphasis original).

The mature Christian leader remains biased toward action. In the final chapter of his book *A Spiritual Clinic*, J. Oswald Sanders paints Caleb the Kenizzite as the Old Testament archetype for lifelong ministry:

> He was spiritually adventurous. "Give me this mountain" (14:12), he demanded. Which mountain? The one where dwelt the fearsome and invincible giants, of course. The mountain which more than forty-five years ago the unhurrying Lord had promised to Caleb and his seed.... His was not careless recklessness but calculating faith. He cherished a godly ambition and would be satisfied with nothing less than the complete fulfillment of the Divine promise. "Give me this mountain" is a grand watchword for the aging Christian.... We can take courage from Caleb. The best lies yet ahead. Caleb never stopped growing because his faith never wavered.... Die climbing![1]

Recall the story I told earlier of my multiday hike through the French Alps. We didn't conquer that strenuous trail by staring at the distant summit; we did it by keeping our eyes on the path right in front of us and plodding forward. That is the essence of a life that leads: simple, repeated faithfulness until you reach your destination.

The mettle required for that lifelong "plodding" is forged in our character. What truly holds many of us back from increasing competence in Christian work isn't a lack of technical training but a failure to develop our character. A leader's walk with God must remain dynamic. We must seek personal growth in every stage of life. While we don't directly determine the scope of the ministry God entrusts to us, we can choose to be earnest and faithful with the opportunities we have been given. We also must learn to adapt and follow the leading of the Holy Spirit in each of life's varied seasons.

The Path of Fulfillment

The promise of character change isn't just greater ministry output. God utterly enriches our inner lives through walking in the Spirit. "So I say, walk by the Spirit … the fruit of the Spirit is love, joy, peace, forbearance, kindness, goodness, faithfulness, gentleness and self-control. Against such things there is no law" (Galatians 5:16, 22–23).

I can honestly say the longer I have followed God, the happier I have been. However, I wouldn't say my life is any easier. In fact, in many ways it's become much harder. Some of this hardship has been induced by my commitment to Christ. But the bulk of it has come in the normal course of life in a broken world.

From where, then, does increasing joy and satisfaction spring? There is no doubt in my mind: Fulfillment and peace come through ever-increasing closeness with God, not through wealth, health, or control.

Walking with God over time produces humility. In a fallen world, humility is a necessary ingredient for happiness. The universe won't conform to our expectations. So, as God humbles us, our chances of enjoying life on earth, despite our trials, dramatically increases. Since God promises increasing growth and fulfillment, it should be thrilling to know we have many miles to go!

Pursuing Christ, Impacting Others

When we commit to pursuing Christ, the results are undeniable. Far from being monkish or inward, true Christian growth causes us to look outward. We grow indeed, but not just for our own sake. We start yearning to better reflect God's love and truth to the world. As God transforms us, we can trust him to make us more effective servants. At a minimum, spiritual leaders model transformed character in compelling ways. But authentic character development should also drive us to become more humble, teachable, and ultimately more skillful in how we love and serve.

My prayer is that in these pages you have uncovered fresh motivation to grow in Christlike character and become a more competent Christian servant. I also hope that as you disciple others, you will prioritize their character. There are many stages to disciple-making, each requiring different skills, and these are detailed in appendix three. Regardless of our approach, we will never produce true leaders if we don't orient our disciples toward the ultimate goal of becoming like Christ. This is the culminating vision of a life that leads: a person so utterly given to Christ that their very existence points toward him.

Take this moment to pray and invite God to make you into whatever he desires, allowing your life to become the living example of the discipleship you hope to see reproduced in others. Make no mistake: "We are God's handiwork, created in Christ Jesus to do good works, which God prepared in advance for us to do" (Ephesians 2:10). He loves you and calls you. He will continue to form you! "He who began a good work in you will carry it on to completion until the day of Christ Jesus" (Philippians 1:6).

Afterword

As you turn the final pages of *A Life That Leads*, you cannot help but sense that Josh Benadum has given us something far more than a leadership manual. He has offered a deeply pastoral invitation. This book reminds us that leadership is not an exclusive realm for a select few. It is a calling woven into the very identity of every disciple of Jesus. Josh captures this beautifully, and he does so with clarity, conviction, and a gentle nudge toward the kind of life that truly influences others.

We live in a world that often measures leadership by platform size, title, or charismatic gifts. I feel that pull at times, and I imagine you do as well. It is easy to admire the generals and forget the foot soldiers, to celebrate the CEO and overlook the steady, faithful neighbor whose quiet obedience shapes lives in ways no spotlight ever could. Josh helps us recover the biblical truth that leadership begins not with a role but with a relationship. We lead well only as we follow Jesus daily and become more like him. Men and women who pursue Christ in this way are deeply transformed, and their lives naturally draw others toward the source of that transformation.

One of the great strengths of this book is how it reframes the entire conversation about spiritual influence. The early church did not transform the Roman Empire by staging grand events or elevating public personalities. They changed the world one household, one friendship, one marketplace conversation at a time. Their power did not come from their titles but from the compelling reality of Christ alive in them. Josh calls us back to that same vision. This is discipleship as Jesus intended it. This is how the gospel continues to spread today, across cultures and generations.

Page after page, Josh offers not only a vision but also a clear pathway. These lessons form a road map for living out the Great Commission through the ordinary rhythms of life. He shows us how character and competence grow together, how abiding in Christ anchors our impact, and how small, faithful steps shape a life of influence that endures. His writing is rooted in Scripture and enriched by real ministry experience, and he invites readers into the kind of spiritual maturity that produces genuine transformation in others.

The vision of this book is a world impacted by authentic disciples permeating every sector of society. The challenge is to release the world's definition of success and embrace the humble, consistent pursuit of Jesus. And the promise is powerful. As you do, your life will carry a ripple effect that is impossible to ignore. Christ will shape you; and through you, others will grow toward maturity in him.

So do not wait for a bigger platform or a special moment. Your life right now is the platform God has entrusted to you. Leadership is for the everyday believer. It belongs to the mother praying over her children, the father guiding his family with patience, the student choosing integrity when it is costly, the teacher who nurtures a struggling learner, the entrepreneur who leads with Christlike ethics, the pastor shepherding a small flock, and the neighbor who practices genuine kindness. These are the lives that shape families, communities, and nations.

Take the truth and tools Josh has given you and step forward in faith. Let your life point others to Jesus. Look for simple, practical ways to make disciples who will turn and do the same.

Go now and live a life that leads.

Rev. Joseph W. Handley, Jr., PhD
CEO, A3; catalyst for leader development, Lausanne Movement

Appendix 1

Character Requirements for Leaders
and All Believers

The biblical standard for leaders is essentially the standard for all believers. The vast majority of qualities required of leaders are found throughout Scripture as the ethical duty of *all* Christians. Leaders therefore aren't called to a categorically higher spiritual tier but a recognition that they are men and women of *proven* Christian character. They have demonstrated maturity and strength in the character qualities toward which all believers should strive.

The purpose of this appendix is to demonstrate this continuity by comparing the New Testament qualifications for leaders with ethical requirements for all believers found throughout Scripture. To maximize readability and utility, this appendix primarily presents parallels without commentary. Where the parallel is ambiguous, key words have been bolded, or brief explanatory notes have been added. Lexical references were taken from Colin Brown's *New International Dictionary of New Testament Theology*[1] and Gerhard Kittel's *Theological Dictionary of the New Testament*.[2]

Passage(s) Relating to Leadership	Parallel Passage(s) Relating to All Believers
"Blameless" Titus 1:6, 7; 1 Timothy 3:2	1 Peter 2:20—"But how is it to your credit if you receive a beating for doing wrong and endure it? But if you suffer for doing good and you endure it, this is commendable before God."
	2 Peter 3:14—"So then, dear friends, since you are looking forward to this, make every effort to be found spotless, blameless and at peace with him."
	Proverbs 5:8—"Keep to a path far from her [the adulteress], do not go near the door of her house."
"Faithful to his wife" Titus 1:6; 1 Timothy 3:2	NOTE: Here Christ makes his argument for marital and sexual ethics using the foundational model of Adam and Eve. Matthew 19:3–6—"Some Pharisees came to him to test him. They asked, 'Is it lawful for a man to divorce his wife for any and every reason?' 'Haven't you read,' he replied, 'that at the beginning the Creator "made them male and female," and said, "For this reason a man will leave his father and mother and be united to his wife, and the two will become one flesh"? So they are no longer two, but one flesh. Therefore what God has joined together, let no one separate.'"
	1 Corinthians 6:18—"Flee from sexual immorality. All other sins a person commits are outside the body, but whoever sins sexually, sins against their own body."

Passage(s) Relating to Leadership	Parallel Passage(s) Relating to All Believers
"Whose children believe and are not open to the charge of being wild and disobedient" Titus 1:6; 1 Timothy 3:4–5	Colossians 3:20–21—"Children, obey your parents in everything, for this pleases the Lord. Fathers, do not embitter your children, or they will become discouraged."
"Not self-willed Titus 1:7 NASB1995	NOTE: Peter represents self-will here as being morally problematic in general, a quality of the unrighteous who will come under God's judgment. 2 Peter 2:9–10—"The Lord knows how to rescue the godly from temptation, and to keep the unrighteous under punishment for the day of judgment, and especially those who indulge the flesh in *its* corrupt desires and despise authority. Daring, **self-willed**, they do not tremble when they revile angelic majesties" (NASB1995, emphasis original).
"Not quick-tempered; peaceable" [lit. not a fighter] Titus 1:7; 1 Timothy 3:3 NASB1995	Galatians 5:19–20—"The acts of the flesh are obvious: sexual immorality, impurity and debauchery; idolatry and witchcraft; hatred, discord, jealousy, **fits of rage**, selfish ambition, dissensions, factions."
	Titus 3:1–2—"Remind the people to be subject to rulers and authorities, to be obedient, to be ready to do whatever is good, to slander no one, to be peaceable and considerate, and always to be gentle toward everyone."

Passage(s) Relating to Leadership	Parallel Passage(s) Relating to All Believers
	Ephesians 4:31–32—"Get rid of all bitterness, rage and anger, brawling and slander, along with every form of malice. Be kind and compassionate to one another, forgiving each other, just as in Christ God forgave you."
	Proverbs 12:16—"Fools show their annoyance at once, but the prudent overlook an insult."
"Not given to drunkenness" Titus 1:7; 1 Timothy 3:3	Ephesians 5:18—"Do not get drunk on wine, which leads to debauchery. Instead, be filled with the Spirit."
	Romans 13:13—"Let us behave decently, as in the daytime, not in carousing and drunkenness, not in sexual immorality and debauchery, not in dissension and jealousy."
	Proverbs 23:20–21—"Do not join those who drink too much wine or gorge themselves on meat, for drunkards and gluttons become poor, and drowsiness clothes them in rags."
"Not violent" [lit., not "striker," not given to physical violence] Titus 1:7; 1 Timothy 3:3	Proverbs 3:31—"Do not envy the violent or choose any of their ways."
	Galatians 5:19–20—"The acts of the flesh are obvious: sexual immorality, impurity and debauchery; idolatry and witchcraft; hatred, discord, jealousy, fits of rage, selfish ambition, dissensions, factions."
	Cf. Cain in Genesis 4; Christ's response in Matthew 26:52 to Peter's attack on Malchus.

Passage(s) Relating to Leadership	Parallel Passage(s) Relating to All Believers
"Not pursuing dishonest gain; not a lover of money" Titus 1:7; 1 Timothy 3:3, 8 (of deacons)	1 Timothy 6:9–10—"Those who want to get rich fall into temptation and a trap and into many foolish and harmful desires that plunge people into ruin and destruction. For the love of money is a root of all kinds of evil. Some people, eager for money, have wandered from the faith and pierced themselves with many griefs."
	Cf. Luke 12:13–34—Parable of the Rich Fool and subsequent teaching.
	Cf. Matthew 18:17—To be a tax collector (i.e., the ultimate example of sordid gain and love of money) is so sinful as to be virtually outside of God's community.
"Hospitable" Titus 1:8; 1 Timothy 3:2	Hebrews 13:2—"Do not forget to show hospitality to strangers, for by so doing some people have shown hospitality to angels without knowing it."
	1 Peter 4:9—"Offer hospitality to one another without grumbling."
"Loves what is good" Titus 1:8	Romans 12:9—"Love must be sincere. Hate what is evil; cling to what is good."
	Matthew 7:17—"Every good tree bears good fruit, but a bad tree bears bad fruit."
	Galatians 6:9–10—"Let us not become weary in doing good, for at the proper time we will reap a harvest if we do not give up. Therefore, as we have opportunity, let us do good to all people, especially to those who belong to the family of believers."

Passage(s) Relating to Leadership	Parallel Passage(s) Relating to All Believers
	Philippians 4:8—"Finally, brothers and sisters, whatever is true, whatever is noble, whatever is right, whatever is pure, whatever is lovely, whatever is admirable—if anything is excellent or praiseworthy—think about such things."
"Sensible" Titus 1:8 NASB1995; 1 Timothy 3:2 CSB	Titus 2:2—"Older men are to be temperate, dignified, sensible, sound in faith, in love, in perseverance" (NASB1995).
	Titus 2:6—"Likewise urge the young men to be sensible" (NASB1995).
	Note: Older women are to teach younger women to be sensible, implying that they too should be sensible. Titus 2:3–5—"Older women likewise are to be reverent in their behavior, not malicious gossips nor enslaved to much wine, teaching what is good, so that they may encourage the young women to love their husbands, to love their children, *to be* **sensible**, pure, workers at home, kind, being subject to their own husbands, so that the word of God will not be dishonored" (NASB1995, emphasis original).
"Just" Titus 1:8 NASB1995	James 2:1–4—"My brothers and sisters, believers in our glorious Lord Jesus Christ must not show favoritism. Suppose a man comes into your meeting wearing a gold ring and fine clothes, and a poor man in filthy old clothes also comes in. If you show special attention to the man wearing fine clothes and say, 'Here's a good seat for you,' but say to the poor man, 'You stand there' or 'Sit on the floor by my feet,' have you not discriminated among yourselves and become judges with evil thoughts?"

Passage(s) Relating to Leadership	Parallel Passage(s) Relating to All Believers
	Note: Paul's ethical teaching is contextualized to the Roman social and economic structures that were common at the time. Slavery was prevalent, and so Paul speaks here to how the gospel ought to transform the personal and economic relationship between masters and slaves. Colossians 4:1—"Masters, provide your slaves with what is right and fair, because you know that you also have a Master in heaven."
	Cf. Matthew 1:19—"And Joseph her husband, being a **righteous** man and not wanting to disgrace her, planned to send her away secretly" (NASB1995).
"Holy" Titus 1:8	Ephesians 4:22, 24—"You were taught … to put on the new self, created to be like God in true righteousness and **holiness**."
"Self-controlled" Titus 1:8 NASB1995	Note: This quality offers a perfect tension to "not self-willed." We should have control over our passions, while in submission to Christ. Galatians 5:22–23—"But the fruit of the Spirit is love, joy, peace, forbearance, kindness, goodness, faithfulness, gentleness and **self-control**. Against such things there is no law."
"Hold firmly to the trustworthy message as it has been taught" Titus 1:9; 1 Timothy 3:9 (of deacons)	Colossians 2:6—"Just as you received Christ Jesus as Lord, continue to live your lives in him."
	1 Timothy 6:3—"If **anyone** teaches otherwise and does not agree to the sound instruction of our Lord Jesus Christ and to godly teaching, they are conceited and understand nothing."

Passage(s) Relating to Leadership	Parallel Passage(s) Relating to All Believers
	Romans 16:17—"I urge you, **brothers and sisters**, to watch out for those who cause divisions and put obstacles in your way that are contrary to the teaching you have learned. Keep away from them."
	2 John 1:9—"**Anyone** who runs ahead and does not continue in the teaching of Christ does not have God; whoever continues in the teaching has both the Father and the Son."
	Cf. Galatians 1:6–9.
"Gentle" 1 Timothy 3:3	Philippians 4:5—"Let your gentleness be evident to all. The Lord is near."
	James 3:17—"But the wisdom from above is first pure, then peaceable, gentle, reasonable, full of mercy and good fruits, unwavering, without hypocrisy" (NASB1995).
"Temperate" 1 Timothy 3:2	Titus 2:2—"Teach the older men to be temperate, worthy of respect, self-controlled, and sound in faith, in love and in endurance."
"Respectable" [lit. orderly; connotes heedful, well-mannered] 1 Timothy 3:2, 7	Proverbs 14:15–16—"The simple believe anything, but the prudent give thought to their steps. The wise fear the Lord and shun evil, but a fool is hotheaded and yet feels secure."
	1 Thessalonians 4:11–12—"Make it your ambition to lead a quiet life: You should mind your own business and work with your hands, just as we told you, so that your daily life may win the respect of outsiders and so that you will not be dependent on anybody."

Passage(s) Relating to Leadership	Parallel Passage(s) Relating to All Believers
"Not conceited" 1 Timothy 3:6	Luke 18:14—"I tell you that this man, rather than the other, went home justified before God. For all those who exalt themselves will be humbled, and those who humble themselves will be exalted."
	2 Timothy 3:1–4—"But mark this: There will be terrible times in the last days. People will be lovers of themselves, lovers of money, boastful, proud, abusive, disobedient to their parents, ungrateful, unholy, without love, unforgiving, slanderous, without self-control, brutal, not lovers of the good, treacherous, rash, **conceited**, lovers of pleasure rather than lovers of God."
"Good reputation with outsiders" 1 Timothy 3:7	Colossians 4:5—"Be wise in the way you act toward outsiders; make the most of every opportunity."
	1 Peter 2:12—"Live such good lives among the pagans that, though they accuse you of doing wrong, they may see your good deeds and glorify God on the day he visits us."
"Able to teach" 1 Timothy 3:2	Matthew 28:19–20—"Therefore go and make disciples of all nations, baptizing them in the name of the Father and of the Son and of the Holy Spirit, and **teaching them to obey** everything I have commanded you."

Appendix 2

Focused Abiding

There is no spiritual discipline requiring more ongoing mainte-nance than regular time spent sitting with and relating to God. Life crowds out our best attempts to give him undivided attention. At times, every believer will have to remove distractions, put their phone away, and humbly reorient themselves toward God's presence. Once our existential connection is restored, spiritual life flows back in. However, starting or restarting times of focused abiding can be difficult. Andrew Murray (1828–1917), a South African pastor renowned for his teachings on the inner life, provides steps below that form an excellent guide for taking your seat before the Lord and returning to his presence, no matter how far your attention has drifted. I recommend mulling over these points daily before moving on to Scripture reading and prayer.

Daily Fellowship with God[1]

1. The first and chief need of our Christian life is, Fellowship with God. The Divine life within us comes from God, and

is entirely dependent upon Him. As I need every moment afresh the air to breathe, as the sun every moment afresh sends down its light, so it is only in direct living communication with God that my soul can be strong. The manna of one day was corrupt when the next day came. I must every day have fresh grace from heaven, and I obtain it only in direct waiting upon God Himself. Begin each day by tarrying before God, and letting Him touch you. Take time to meet God.

2.   To this end, let your first act in your devotion be a setting yourself still before God. In prayer, or worship, everything depends upon God taking the chief place. I must bow quietly before Him in humble faith and adoration, speaking thus within my heart: "God is. God is near. God is love, longing to communicate Himself to me. God the Almighty One, Who works all in all, is even now waiting to work in me, and make Himself known." Take time, till you know God is very near.

3.   When you have given God His place of honor, glory, and power, take your place of deepest lowliness, and seek to be filled with the Spirit of humility. As a creature it is your blessedness to be nothing, that God may be all in you. As a sinner you are not worthy to look up to God; bow in self-abasement. As a saint, let God's love overwhelm you, and bow you still lower down. Sink down before Him in humility, meekness, patience, and surrender to His goodness and mercy. He will exalt you. Oh! take time, to get very low before God.

4.   Then accept and value your place in Christ Jesus. God delights in nothing but His beloved Son, and can be satisfied with nothing else in those who draw nigh to Him.

Enter deep into God's holy presence in the boldness which the blood gives, and in the assurance that in Christ you are most well-pleasing. In Christ you are within the veil. You have access into the very heart and love of the Father. This is the great object of fellowship with God, that I may have more of God in my life, and that God may see Christ formed in me. Be silent before God and let Him bless you.

5. This Christ is a living Person. He loves you with a personal love, and He looks every day for the personal response of your love. Look into His face with trust, till His love really shines into your heart. Make His heart glad by telling Him that you do love Him. He offers Himself to you as a personal Savior and Keeper from the power of sin. Do not ask, can I be kept from sinning, if I keep close to Him? But ask, can I be kept from sinning, if He always keeps close to me? And you see at once how safe it is to trust Him.

6. We have not only Christ's life in us as a power, and His presence with us as a person, but we have His likeness to be wrought into us. He is to be formed in us, so that His form or figure, His likeness, can be seen in us. Bow before God until you get some sense of the greatness and blessedness of the work to be carried on by God in you this day. Say to God, "Father, here am I for you to give as much in me of Christ's likeness as I can receive." And wait to hear Him say, "My child, I give thee as much of Christ as thy heart is open to receive." The God who revealed Jesus in the flesh and perfected Him, will reveal Him in thee and perfect thee in Him. The Father loves the Son, and delights to work out His image and likeness in thee. Count upon it that this blessed work will be done in thee as thou waitest on thy God, and holdest fellowship with Him.

7. The likeness to Christ consists chiefly in two things—the likeness of His death and resurrection, (Rom. 6:5). The death of Christ was the consummation of His humility and obedience, the entire giving up of His life to God. In Him we are dead to sin. As we sink down in humility and dependence and entire surrender to God, the power of His death works in us, and we are made conformable to His death. And so we know Him in the power of His resurrection, in the victory over sin, and all the joy and power of the risen life. Therefore every morning, "present yourselves unto God as those that are alive from the dead." He will maintain the life He gave, and bestow the grace to live as risen ones.

8. All this can only be in the power of the Holy Spirit, who dwells in you. Count upon Him to glorify Christ in you. Count upon Christ to increase in you the inflowing of His Spirit. As you wait before God to realize His presence, remember that the Spirit is in you to reveal the things of God. Seek in God's presence to have the anointing of the Spirit of Christ so truly that your whole life may every moment be spiritual.

9. As you meditate on this wondrous salvation and seek full fellowship with the great and holy God, and wait on Him to reveal Christ in you, you will feel how needful the giving up of all is to receive Him. Seek grace to know what it means to live as wholly for God as Christ did. Only the Holy Spirit Himself can teach you what an entire yielding of the whole life to God can mean. Wait on God to show you in this what you do not know. Let every approach to God, and every request for fellowship with Him be accompanied by a new, very definite, and entire surrender to Him to work in you.

10. "By faith" must here, as through all Scripture, and all the spiritual life, be the keynote. As you tarry before God, let it be in a deep quiet faith in Him, the Invisible One, who is so near, so holy, so mighty, so loving. In a deep, restful faith too, that all the blessings and powers of the heavenly life are around you, and in you. Just yield yourself in the faith of a perfect trust to the Ever Blessed Holy Trinity to work out all God's purpose in you. Begin each day thus in fellowship with God, and God will be all in all to you.

Appendix 3

Stages of Disciple-Making

Much of this book has focused on growing in Christlikeness and cultivating the core competencies that define effective leadership. However, the ultimate measure of true leadership is not what you accomplish alone, but what you reproduce in others. A leader's greatest legacy is defined by their capacity for multiplication. The stages of disciple-making place emphasis on the relational process of helping others follow and grow. This is the heart of disciple-making.

As the foundation of Christian leadership, disciple-making is a biblical priority as well as a contextual practice. What this means is that while Jesus' call to "go and make disciples" is universal and relevant to all Christians, in practice it can and should vary, depending on the environment.

Jim Putman and Bobby Harrington capture the broadness of disciple-making in their book *DiscipleShift*, defining it as "entering into relationships to help people trust and follow Jesus (Matthew 28:18–20), which includes the whole process from conversion through maturation and multiplication."[1] Understood this way, disciple-making includes sharing the gospel, teaching the Bible, loving and serving, helping people grow in character—and most other forms of personal ministry.

Now compare Putnam and Harrington's definition with this one, taken from the training materials of a discipleship-focused church in the United States: "A [disciple-maker] is one who helps willing people attain Deacon Team status by both ministering in a general way in the church, and by holding specific meetings for study, coaching, counseling, and prayer."

The differences between these two definitions are starkly apparent. The church training definition is highly prescriptive and organizationally focused. It sets the specific, measurable goal of disciple-making as achieving an organizational rank ("Deacon Team status"), and identifies the means to that end.

Conversely, Putnam and Harrington's view is significantly broader. Almost any type of ministry could count as disciple-making.

So which approach is better?

Theologically, the *DiscipleShift* definition aligns with the full biblical mandate. The Great Commission (Matthew 28:19–20) clearly defines the scope of disciple-making: "Therefore go and make disciples of all nations, baptizing them in the name of the Father and of the Son and of the Holy Spirit, and teaching them to obey everything I have commanded you." This passage establishes a dual focus of both conversion (baptism) and training (teaching), showing that disciple-making encompasses both initial conversion and lifelong spiritual growth.

However, this isn't the only verse we have on disciple-making. The New Testament gives us contextual examples as well. For instance, consider 2 Timothy 2:2: "And the things you have heard me say in the presence of many witnesses entrust to reliable people who will also be qualified to teach others." Paul's charge to Timothy suggests that effective disciple-making includes a leadership element. Timothy needed to seek out people who would be qualified in character (reliable) and able to multiply.

Overall, I believe it's helpful (and biblical) to view disciple-making as involving many overlapping stages ranging from pre-conversion engagement all the way to mature Christian leadership. However, if disciple-making is to be effective, leaders must articulate clear, best practices and communal norms within each of these different stages.

The Stages of Disciple-Making: A Goal-Oriented Framework

The process of discipleship is reflected in the pyramid diagram below, where the left side outlines the disciple's progression (Seeking, Converting, etc.), and the right side outlines the corresponding active role of the disciple-maker (Witnessing, Baptizing, etc.).

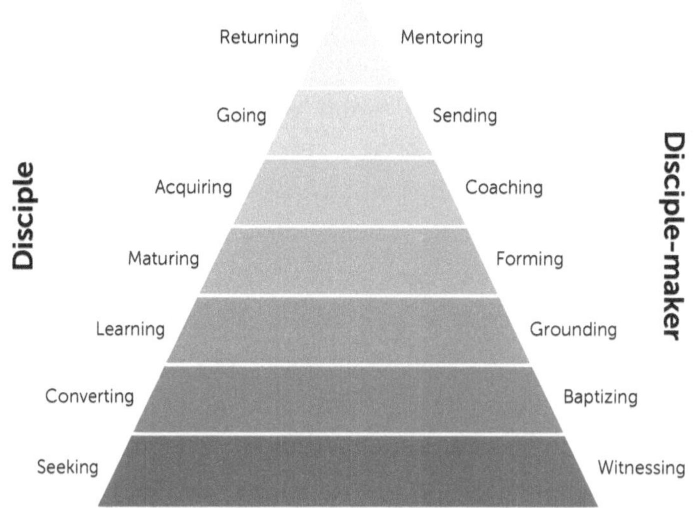

Dysfunction tends to emerge when either the disciple or the disciple-maker attempts to move up or down the pyramid without the cooperation of the other. The pyramid's natural narrowing as it ascends reflects Jesus' teaching on "the narrow road" (Matthew 7:13–14; see also James 3:1). In practical terms, we will always baptize and ground far more people than we will coach and send.

The discipleship process is often non-linear, and many stages overlap. Forming and Coaching ministry, for instance, are almost always concurrent. Similarly, Grounding (laying spiritual foundations) at times needs to be revisited. After all, if you are building a house and discover large cracks in the foundation, then all other work must pause until you've had a chance to dig back down and reinforce. The same is true when it comes to disciple-making.

Stage 1: Witnessing

The first stage of disciple-making according to this paradigm is **Seeking/Witnessing**. This is largely what Christians refer to as "evangelism." It involves sharing the good news of Jesus, demonstrating the love and power of the Holy Spirit, and addressing personal, cultural, and intellectual barriers to faith.

Disciple-Maker Goals for this Stage: These include building trust relationships and exposing the person to spiritual community where they can hear God's truth and also see it lived out. Disciple-makers are more effective at witnessing when they are equipped to answer people's questions about Christianity. They must also know Scripture well enough to explain its meaning. Friendship-building is another essential skill during this stage. Few people will see success in witnessing if they lack the ability to make real friends. Time investment during this stage, however, is often irregular. Rarely does someone want to study the Bible weekly when they haven't yet received the Holy Spirit. So, disciple-makers do their best to meet people at their current level of interest, all the while praying that God would soften their heart and open their eyes to truth (2 Corinthians 4:4). If a person is a seeker, then Jesus promises they will find the truth (Matthew 7:7).

Stage 2: Baptizing

The **Converting/Baptizing** stage happens when a person turns their heart to Jesus and admits their need for his gift of grace. They are spiritually baptized into him through the indwelling of the Holy Spirit—something later to be publicly symbolized with water.

Disciple-Maker Goals for this Stage: This includes helping the person reach the point of decision, by asking questions like, "What else is holding you back from putting your trust in Jesus?" We also ought to help individuals grapple with the implications of receiving Jesus as their Lord and Savior—since it will result in a radical reorientation in their life.

Stage 3: Grounding

Once a disciple has passed from spiritual death to new life in Christ (Ephesians 2:1–10), spiritual growth can finally begin. This should inaugurate a **Learning/Grounding** phase. Because spiritual foundations are essential, we must be committed to helping new believers and establish them strongly from the outset. It's perilous to rush the basics of Christian growth— things like identity, prayer, Scripture, community, and service. New believers also need to be aware of the spiritual battlefield— specifically the menace that Satan represents to their spiritual lives. They must be actively prepared to face new levels of temptation and learn how to deal with their sin while embracing God's abundant grace.

Disciple-Maker Goals for this Stage: Beginning to meet regularly at this point is often both realistic and beneficial, much like establishing a routine for meaningful progress in any other pursuit. This regular time with a disciple should cultivate both deep friendship and foundational habits. Most of the time should be spent growing the relationship, talking about life, praying together, and studying Scripture. One of the men who discipled me said he refused to study anything but Scripture with new Christians for a full year after they come to faith. There are many good books out there on apologetics and leadership. But there is simply no replacement for the "pure spiritual milk" of God's Word in helping people to reach maturity (1 Peter 2:2).

Stage 4: Maturing

The **Maturing/Forming** stage extends beyond just basic learning to developing deep and stable biblical convictions. The now well-rooted believer begins experiencing significant inner transformation, making a godly lifestyle both possible and sustainable.

It's impossible for this part of the process to happen just through study and conversation. Personal failure and suffering are often needed gateways to formation-level change. Most people need to go through a period of dissonance where they are less sustained by the excitement of initial spiritual experiences and new relationships. God in his wisdom allows people to struggle and come to meaningful forks in the road where they must make big faith decisions.

Disciple-Maker Goals for this Stage: We must be eager to guide our friends through these important challenges, recognizing that what happens at these key junctures can set the tone, pace, and ceiling for everything that comes after. Therefore, we should offer consistent encouragement and loving correction when necessary.

We also need to develop the key skill of effective modeling. We can say with Paul, "Follow my example, as I follow the example of Christ" (1 Corinthians 11:1), but living in a deliberately accessible, compelling, and imitable way is far from simple. Humility, for instance, is a virtue that can be described with words but remains mysteriously abstract until demonstrated in tangible situations. Wisdom and discernment are also intensely practical qualities. For this reason, the effectiveness of disciple-makers who try to disciple from a thousand feet will be limited. We need to let people into our thoughts, struggles, successes, and relationships to the degree that they can truly see Christ in us and learn by example how to involve him deeply in their own lives.

Stage 5: Coaching

Coaching, in this stage, means actively training and empowering the disciple to move from simple forms of reactionary serving to intentional ministry efforts, thereby multiplying their spiritual influence. **Acquiring/Coaching** is perhaps the most overlapping of all seven stages. It ought to accompany almost every other stage, following conversion/baptism. This is because even young believers should be encouraged to find ways to serve and do ministry. Of course, more sophisticated leadership roles should require a certain character and experience. But anyone who has God's Spirit is automatically given gifts to build up others in the church (1 Corinthians 12:7).

Disciple-Maker Goals for this Stage: Disciple-makers increase their time commitment to intentionally coaching and helping disciples develop ministry skills only once they are clearly well grounded in the faith and beginning to mature. Focusing too quickly on "doing" can lead to missed core learning. As we have explored throughout this book, real and lasting fruitfulness isn't just a matter of ability but requires cultivating a posture of humble abiding (John 15:1–5). When we are assured of a disciple's spiritual foundations, we can more confidently equip and empower them to lead, accepting that mistakes and setbacks will be part of the process.

The principal goal for this stage is seeing our friends begin to make disciples themselves, fulfilling Paul's call to Timothy to "entrust to reliable people *who will also be qualified to teach others*" (2 Timothy 2:2). We should hope to see disciples participate in leading others to faith in Jesus and take responsibility for helping them grow. This is an exciting season, and often the time when people's primary spiritual giftings become apparent.

Confident disciple-makers are quick to empower disciples and help them find meaningful opportunities for spiritual leadership. It's important, however, to maintain a shared ministry context as much as possible, so you can keep learning and serving together. Paul believed in Timothy but also kept him close until he was finally ready to go off on his own to lead the church in Ephesus.

Stage 6: Sending

Paul did eventually let Timothy go. Effective disciple-making inevitably leads to **Going/Sending**. Disciple-making is never about gathering people to ourselves. It's about lovingly walking alongside them, doing all we can to help them be faithful and fruitful in Christ. Similar to raising healthy children, disciples must outgrow us and our direct influence. The timing of this depends largely on the person's pace of growth and spiritual opportunities, which could include the disciple moving on to another ministry, stepping into a new leadership role, or entering a season of life where they no longer have time or need to meet with us in the same capacity.

Disciple-Maker Goals for this Stage: When experienced disciple-makers sense sending is near, they amp up encouragement and take every opportunity to present "capstone training" (final, intensive training focused on synthesizing knowledge and preparing for leadership challenges). Key examples of this focused preparation can be found in Paul's address to the Ephesian elders in Acts 20, or the final chapter of 2 Timothy. It's important we send people out with our love, confidence, and full support. By this stage, they should be independent thinkers and self-motivated learners, fully capable of acting as spiritual pillars to those around them.

This can be a thrilling but also sad moment, representing the passing of a season and change in an important relationship. But we do it all the same, knowing the reward in heaven will outweigh the relational sacrifices we make now. It's important to mark this stage with some sort of commendation or celebration, affirming our love and commitment to keep praying for this person even as they go on to bigger and better things.

Stage 7: Mentoring

The final stage is **Returning/Mentoring**. Not everyone we send will necessarily engage in this stage. But as a disciple-maker, we should be prepared and eager to play this role whenever possible. In fact, in later years, after we have discipled many people, this may become a significant part of our ministry. Mentoring is primarily sporadic and reactive in nature. It often involves maintaining a strong trust relationship by simply being available to consult and encourage when needed. If we can successfully maintain this trust, we may be in a crucial position to provide wisdom or intervene in their lives down the road. After all, later stages of life present new challenges that require new learning and spiritual growth. By continuing to mature ourselves, we remain well suited to step back in and counsel our friends through life and ministry when required. What a joy and privilege it is when roles reverse, and we find our disciples have grown alongside and even beyond us, putting us in a position where we might need their help.

Growth in Disciple-Making

One key implication of a "stages" model of disciple-making is that different stages require us to develop new qualities and skills in order to be effective. Some of us have led friends to faith and grounded them in the basics, but we haven't yet seen someone we disciple grow into a spiritual leader who disciples others. While we can only take people as far as they are willing to go, faithfulness in ministry requires a growth mindset. Without taking undue responsibility, we should always be seeking ways to become more effective in serving the Lord.

Common Disciple-Maker Pitfalls

Different common weaknesses can derail a disciple-maker's efforts:

A Lack of Character Focus. Disciple-makers who downplay the importance of character formation will likely see disciples burn out or spin out spiritually. They might be skilled at empowering and equipping but will lose people at critical junctures where patience or nuanced challenge is needed.

An Over-Focus on Devotion. Some disciple-makers have an overly devotional view of spiritual growth. They teach identity truths, prayer, and model a contemplative Christian life, but they lack vision for spiritual leadership or underappreciate the role that competency development plays in people's confidence and motivation.

An Unwillingness to Send. Other disciple-makers are all-in and committed but become possessive and overly prescriptive. Although they can be effective to a degree with more compliant personalities, when it comes time to empower and send, they are either unwilling to do so, or their disciples flounder the moment they step away from the disciple-maker's influence.

Commit to Learning

Improving as a disciple-maker should be a high priority for every one of us. It's both a biblical calling as well as a contextual practice. We discern our disciple-making convictions from the pages of Scripture but also from partnering with others in our local church to figure out how to do so earnestly and effectively.

Imagine for a moment you want to be a guide in the magnificent Olympic National Park in the State of Washington. You could show up in the park tomorrow and start offering your services. You might be able to apply yourself and help a few people. But to be a truly quality guide, you would do much more. You would likely walk the trails to familiarize yourself well with them. You'd probably study guidebooks and maps and research what it means to be a guide. You'd develop wilderness survival skills and maybe take classes. You might even seek out a mentor—an older, more experienced guide to show you the ropes. And you'd probably begin to lead introductory hikes by guiding beginner groups on well-known, safe trails, while you continue your training.

Analogously, we pursue effective disciple-making by doing the same things. We keep growing ourselves by living out a deep faith relationship with God (walking the trails). We study hard (reading spiritual books and Scripture, attending classes). We hang around those with experience and learn everything we can from them (finding mentors). Finally, we don't wait until we are experts, but we apply what we learn in real life. Remember, we don't need to posture ourselves as sages or gurus. We are only those who have gone a little further ahead—dedicated to helping our friends reach new spiritual heights to God's glory.

Actionable Disciple-Making Goals

Use the following table to plan actionable commitments and measurable goals for each stage with individuals you are currently discipling. The Witnessing stage has been filled out as an example.

Stage	DM's Role	DM's Goal-Setting	Measurable Outcomes for the DM
1 Witnessing	Building trust, invitation, and sharing the gospel	Example: I will initiate and schedule two relational points of contact (e.g., coffee, lunch, or a shared hobby activity) within a month. I'll also extend one explicit invitation to a community activity where others express their faith (e.g., a small group community meal or a service project).	The person accepts the invitation to the small group/community activity or agrees to consider a portion of Scripture.
2 Baptizing	Guiding to a decision for Christ		
3 Grounding	Establishing foundational beliefs and habits		

Stage	DM's Role	DM's Goal-Setting	Measurable Outcomes for the DM
4 Forming	Modeling character transformation		
5 Coaching	Equipping for replication		
6 Sending	Releasing to independent mission		
7 Mentoring	Availability and long-term counsel		

Key Resources for Growing as a Disciple-Maker

The Master Plan of Evangelism, by Dr. Robert E. Coleman

Discipling in a Multicultural World, by Ajith Fernando

Organic Discipleship: Mentoring Others Into Spiritual Maturity and Leadership, by Dennis McCallum and Jessica Lowery

The Lost Art of Disciple Making, by Leroy Eims

Notes

Introduction

1. Edward L. Smither, *Mission in the Early Church: Themes and Reflections* (Cascade Books, 2014), Kindle edition, 43–48.

2. Robert Booth, "Young People Becoming Less Happy than Older Generations, Research Shows," *The Guardian*, March 20, 2024, https://www.theguardian.com/society/2024/mar/20/young-people-becoming-less-happy-than-older-generations-research-shows.

1 The Making of a Leader

1. J. Oswald Sanders, *Cultivation of Christian Character* (Moody Publishers, 2012), Kindle edition, 9–10.

2. At the fourth Lausanne Congress in Seoul, South Korea, in September 2024, "developing leaders of character" qualified as one of twenty-five gaps in the Great Commission to be addressed by the global church. I was privileged to be part of these discussions alongside other leaders from around the world. From Finland to Nepal, everyone reported the same thing. Pastors are aging, and there are few strong prospective leaders from emerging generations. All delegates agreed that traditional equipping platforms, such as seminaries, are insufficient. True progress will require contextualized discipleship in the local church.

2 The Goal of the Christian Life

1. Merriam-Webster, s.v. "Character," accessed October 16, 2025, https://www.merriam-webster.com/dictionary/character.

2. Letter to George Steptoe Washington, December 5, 1790, George Washington's Mount Vernon, accessed September 23, 2025, https://www.

mountvernon.org/library/digitalhistory/past-projects/quotes/article/a-good-moral-character-is-the-first-essential-in-a-man-it-is-therefore-highly-important-that-you-should-endeavor-not-only-to-be-learned-but-virtuous.

3   Bruce Lee, *Striking Thoughts: Bruce Lee's Wisdom for Daily Living*, ed. John Little (Tuttle Publishing, 2000), 46.

4   Dietrich Bonhoeffer, "The Day Alone," in *Life Together*, trans. John W. Doberstein (Harper & Row, 1954), 75–89.

5   W. Arndt et al., *A Greek-English Lexicon of the New Testament and Other Early Christian Literature*, 3rd ed. (University of Chicago Press, 2000), 639.

6   Sanders, *Cultivation of Christian Character*, 9–10.

7   John Stott, *The Radical Disciple: Some Neglected Aspects of Our Calling* (IVP Books, 2010), 29.

8   Stott, *The Radical Disciple*, 29.

9   Elisabeth Elliot, *Be Still My Soul: Reflections on Living the Christian Life* (Baker Publishing Group, 2003), Kindle edition, 29.

3   The Leader's Journey

1   Andrew Murray, *The Andrew Murray Collection: 21 Classic Works* (Waxkeep Publishing, 2013), Kindle edition, Kindle location 828–29 of 24613.

2   Corrie ten Boom, *Tramp for the Lord* (Fleming H. Revell, 1974), 113.

3   C. S. Lewis, *Mere Christianity* (HarperCollins, 2001), 103.

4   The Greek word for "save" (σώσω/sodzo) has a broad meaning. See Arndt et al., *A Greek-English Lexicon of the New Testament and Other Early Christian Literature*, 982–83.

5   Watchman Nee, *The Release of the Spirit* (The Sure Foundation, 1965), 9.

6   C. S. Lewis, *Voyage of the Dawn Treader* (HarperCollins, 2002), 87–120.

7   C. S. Lewis, *The Screwtape Letters* (HarperCollins, 2001), 76.

4   Surrendering to God and Others

1   Watchman Nee, *The Normal Christian Worker* (Hong Kong Church Book Room Ltd., 1987), 65.

5   Staying Grounded in Scripture

1   J. Oswald Sanders, *Spiritual Leadership* (Moody Press, 1967), 42.

2   A reference website such as www.biblegateway.com is a useful tool for topical studies.

3   Navigators is a well-established organization that teaches disciple-making

methods. Check out their easy-to-use resources on inductive Bible study: Navigators, "How to Study the Bible," accessed October 20, 2025, https://www.navigators.org/resource/how-to-study-the-bible/.

6 Making Good Decisions

1 Arndt et al., *A Greek-English Lexicon of the New Testament and Other Early Christian Literature*, 987.

2 Arndt et al., *A Greek-English Lexicon of the New Testament and Other Early Christian Literature*, 987.

7 Caring for What Belongs to You

1 Ajith Fernando, *The Family Life of a Christian Leader* (Crossway, 2016), 106–7.

2 For more on qualifications for elders and having believing children, see Justin Taylor, "Unbelief in an Elder's Children," Desiring God, February 1, 2007, https://www.desiringgod.org/articles/unbelief-in-an-elders-children.

8 Cultivating Consistent Zeal

1 Helmut Thielicke, *Encounter with Spurgeon*, trans. John W. Doberstein (Baker, 1977), 81.

2 J. Oswald Sanders, *A Spiritual Clinic: Problems of Christian Discipleship* (Moody Press, 1958), 224.

9 Building a Life of Welcome

1 Bible Hub, s.v. "philoxenos (Strong's 5382)," accessed October 23, 2025, https://biblehub.com/greek/5382.htm.

2 Paul A. Varg, "Motives in Protestant Missions, 1890–1917," *Church History* 23, no. 1 (March 1954): 71.

3 Nee, *The Normal Christian Worker*, 34.

10 Developing Merciful Discernment

1 Arndt et al., *A Greek-English Lexicon of the New Testament and Other Early Christian Literature*, 371.

2 Bill Lawrence, "Foundational Principles of Leadership," *Bible.org*, December 20, 2007, https://bible.org/article/foundational-principles-leadership.

3 Conrad Hilario, *Searching for Wisdom: Finding the Father in Proverbs* (New Paradigm Publishing, Kindle Edition), Kindle location 2256 of 3144.

4   See this excellent teaching from biblical counselor Kalyssa Deken: "Developing Mercy with Discernment," Dwell Community Church, June 17, 2023, https://www.dwellcc.org/teaching/7005/kalyssa-deken/2023/developing-mercy-with-discernment.

11   Transferring Truth Effectively

1   Arndt et al., *A Greek-English Lexicon of the New Testament and Other Early Christian Literature*, 241.

2   See Trevin Wax's article that explores this theme: Trevin Wax, "Discipleship Is More Than Conveying Information" *The Gospel Coalition*, February 9, 2012, https://www.thegospelcoalition.org/blogs/trevin-wax/discipleship-is-more-than-conveying-information/.

3   Thielicke, *Encounter with Spurgeon*, 34.

4   Sanders, *Cultivation of Christian Character*, 15.

5   Timothy Keller, "Ministry and Character," Redeemer City to City, January 1, 2002, https://redeemercitytocity.com/articles-stories/ministry-and-character.

12   Being Honest and Reliable

1   Larry Crabb, *Encouragement: The Unexpected Power of Building Others Up* (Zondervan, 2013), Kindle edition, location 263 of 1924.

2   Bob Sorge, *Dealing with the Rejection and Praise of Man* (Oasis House, 1999).

13   Doing What Is Right

1   Arndt et al., *A Greek-English Lexicon of the New Testament and Other Early Christian Literature*, 246.

14   Soul *and* Skill

1   Merriam-Webster, s.v. "Competence," accessed October 24, 2025, https://www.merriam-webster.com/dictionary/competence.

2   "General George Smith Patton Quotes," Military-Quotes.com, accessed October 6, 2025, https://www.military-quotes.com/Patton.htm.

3   Jeff Cunningham, "Warren Buffett Learned How To Invest When He Figured Out How To Live," Medium, March 30, 2020, https://medium.com/be-somebody/warren-buffetts-three-competencies-opportunity-organization-and-outcomes-2dffe86568d2.

4   Larry J. Michael, *Spurgeon on Leadership: Key Insights for Christian Leaders from the Prince of Preachers* (Kregel Academic, 2010), Kindle edition, Kindle location 110–12 of 2439.

5   Ajith Fernando, *Discipling in a Multicultural World* (Crossway, 2019), Kindle edition, location 637 of 6071.

6   Charles Spurgeon, *An All-Around Ministry: Addresses to Ministers and Students* (Ichthus Publications, 2014), Kindle edition, 173.

7   Brian Sanders, *Microchurches: A Smaller Way* (Underground Media, 2019), Kindle edition, 32.

8   Robert E. Coleman, *The Master Plan of Evangelism* (Revell, 1993), Kindle edition, 107–8.

9   LeRoy Eims, *Be a Motivational Leader: Lasting Leadership Principles* (David C Cook, 2012), Kindle edition, 140.

15 The Traps That Hinder Growth

1   Sanders, *Cultivation of Christian Character*, 14.

2   While burnout can be a symptom of lopsided growth, it can also be a physical, psychological, or organizational issue resulting from poor boundaries, unsustainable workloads, or destructive environments.

3   Sanders, *A Spiritual Clinic*, 62–63.

4   Peter Greer and Chris Horst, *Mission Drift: The Unspoken Crisis Facing Leaders, Charities, and Churches* (Bethany House Publishers, 2014), Kindle edition, 15.

5   Dennis McCallum, *Satan and His Kingdom: What the Bible Says and How It Matters to You* (Bethany House Publishers, 2009), Kindle edition, 160–61.

6   Mark J. Edwards, "Origen," *The Stanford Encyclopedia of Philosophy* (Summer 2022 Edition), ed. Edward N. Zalta, accessed October 6, 2025, https://plato.stanford.edu/archives/sum2022/entries/origen/.

7   Sanders, *Cultivation of Christian Character*, 11.

8   Sanders, *Cultivation of Christian Character*, 25.

9   Corrie ten Boom, with John and Elizabeth Sherrill, *The Hiding Place* (Chosen Books, 2006), 12.

10   Miroslav Volf, *Exclusion and Embrace: A Theological Exploration of Identity, Otherness, and Reconciliation* (Abingdon Press, 1996), 134.

16 The Sustaining Disciplines

1   Matteo, "Meet the 93-Year-Old Marathoner Redefining What Aging Looks Like," *The Running Week*, July 22, 2025, https://www.therunningweek.com/post/meet-the-93-year-old-marathoner-redefining-what-aging-looks-like.

2   Francis A. Schaeffer, *The God Who Is There* (InterVarsity Press, 1968), 139.

3   Watchman Nee, *Sit, Walk, Stand* (Tyndale House, 1977), 34.

[4] Mark Sayers, *Reappearing Church: The Hope for Renewal in the Rise of Our Post-Christian Culture* (Moody Publishers, 2019), Kindle edition, 151.

[5] Bonhoeffer, *Life Together*, 17.

[6] Fernando, *Discipling in a Multicultural World*, Kindle location 839 of 6071.

[7] Randy Alcorn, *Managing God's Money: A Biblical Guide* (Tyndale House Publishers, 2011), Kindle edition, 24.

[8] Alcorn, *Managing God's Money*, 48.

[9] Nancy Leigh DeMoss, *Choosing Gratitude: Your Journey to Joy* (Moody Publishers, 2009), 13–14.

[10] Gary DeLashmutt, *Colossians: Christ Over All; Christ In You* (New Paradigm Publishing, 2016), Kindle edition, 112.

Conclusion

[1] Sanders, *A Spiritual Clinic*, 227–29.

Appendix 1

[1] Colin Brown, ed., *The New International Dictionary of New Testament Theology*, 4 vols. (Zondervan, 1986), Logos Bible Software edition.

[2] Gerhard Kittel and Gerhard Friedrich, eds., *Theological Dictionary of the New Testament*, trans. and ed. Geoffrey W. Bromiley, 10 vols. (Wm. B. Eerdmans, 1976), Logos Bible Software edition.

Appendix 2

[1] Taken from Andrew Murray, *The Deeper Christian Life: An Aid to Its Attainment* (Fleming H. Revell, 1895), 5–10.

Appendix 3

[1] Jim Putman and Bobby Harrington, with Robert E. Coleman, *Discipleshift: Five Steps That Help Your Church Make Disciples Who Make Disciples* (Zondervan, 2013), 43.

Acknowledgments

This book wouldn't have come together if it weren't for the amazing team at 100Movements, especially Anna Robinson. She was a wonderful partner in shaping the content and tone, truly a master of her craft.

There isn't enough space to recognize all the authors, mentors, and friends who gave me help and feedback over the years to get to this point. But Pat Reeder, Dennis McCallum, Caleb Benadum, Tim Benadum, Marjie Benadum, Meri Benadum, Barb King, Hannah O'Malley, Mark Bowes, Brian Sanders, Gary DeLashmutt, Bev DeLashmutt, Sean Richards, Conrad Hilario, Dave Glover, Mike Sullivan, Bret McCallum, and John Ross are all fantastic folks who contributed significantly in one way or another.

About the Author

Josh grew up on the mission field in Phnom Penh, Cambodia. He moved to the States in 2006 to go to college, where he met his wife, Meri. Together they began leading and planting house churches, and this remains their primary ministry. Josh has pastored in large church settings but now serves Acacia House Churches in Orlando, Florida. He also coaches church planters with Stadia Church Planting and coordinates Brave Future, a collective of microchurch movements. He and Meri have three amazing children and are dedicated to making disciples in every place God sends them.

Discover more resources and connect with Josh by going to https://joshbenadum.substack.com/ or scanning the QR code below.

www.ingramcontent.com/pod-product-compliance
Lightning Source LLC
Chambersburg PA
CBHW030919060726
47591CB00005B/1600